Basic Bible Sermons on Handling Conflict

262.5
Pow

BASIC BIBLE SERMONS ON HANDLING CONFLICT

Paul W. Powell

BROADMAN PRESS
NASHVILLE, TENNESSEE

© Copyright 1992 • Broadman Press
All rights reserved

4222-79
ISBN: 0-8054-2279-X

Dewey Decimal Classification: 262.5
Subject Heading: CHURCH - SERMONS
Library of Congress Catalog Card Number: 91-34556
Printed in the United States of America

All Scripture quotations are from the *King James Version* of the Bible. Scripture quotations marked (NIV) are from THE HOLY BIBLE; *New International Version* © 1973, 1978, 1984 by International Bible Society.

Library of Congress Cataloging-in-Publication Data

Powell, Paul W.
  Basic Bible sermons on handling conflict / Paul W. Powell.
    p.   cm. — (Basic Bible sermons series)
  ISBN 0-8054-2279-X
  1. Conflict management in the Bible—Sermons. 2. Reconciliation—Sermons. 3. Sermons, American. 4. Southern Baptist Convention—Sermons. 5. Baptists—Sermons. I. Title. II. Series.
BS680.C63P68 1992
250—dc20
                                                                    91-34556
                                                                    CIP

This book is dedicated to the employees of the Annuity Board, who help to keep me out of conflict.

Other Books in the Basic Bible Sermons Series:

Basic Bible Sermons on the Cross, W. A. Criswell
Basic Bible Sermons on Psalms for Everyday Living,
    James T. Draper, Jr.
Basic Bible Sermons on Hope, David Albert Farmer
Basic Bible Sermons on Philippians, J. B. Fowler
Basic Bible Sermons on John, Herschel H. Hobbs
Basic Bible Sermons on Easter, Chevis F. Horne
Basic Bible Sermons on Christmas, Chevis F. Horne
Basic Bible Sermons on Spiritual Living, Stephen B. McSwain
Basic Bible Sermons on Christian Stewardship,
    J. Alfred Smith, Sr., with J. Alfred Smith, Jr.
Basic Bible Sermons on the Church, Ralph Smith
Basic Bible Sermons on the Ten Commandments, Jerry Vines

Contents

Introduction	ix
1. The Church in Travail	11
2. Facing Conflict Within	20
3. Obstacles to Taking the Promised Land	32
4. Conflict Over Leadership	46
5. When Workers Can't Work Together	59
6. Spillover Conflict	71
7. When Others Hurt You	80
8. Working Out Doctrinal Differences	88
9. Bloom Where You Are Planted	98
10. Shake the Dust from Your Feet	110
11. Working with Other Denominations Than Yours	119

Introduction

When Christ established His church, His purpose was clear. We were to be His witnesses to the ends of the earth. This main purpose of the church represents the will of God. It is His desire that all men might be reconciled to Himself through Christ.

Thus God has committed the "ministry of reconciliation" to His church. Unfortunately, some churches have come to represent the forces of alienation rather than reconciliation. Division, schism, and conflict plague many congregations today.

Having lost their vision of the nature and the purpose of the church, many congregations are characterized by seething anger, destructive relationships, mistrust of leaders, and unmet personal needs.

At youth camp I used to enjoy singing the song, *"The Old Time Religion."* One of my favorite verses was the one that went:

> It makes the Baptist love the Methodist
> It makes the Baptist love the Methodist
> It makes the Baptist love the Methodist
> It's good enough for me.

Somehow there must come an extensive healing in the church before there can be a recovery of vision. We must hear again and begin to take seriously the prayer of Jesus for His church, "[I pray for these . . .] That they may be one; as thou, Father, art in me, and I in thee, that they also may be one in us: *that the world may believe thou hast sent me*" (John 17:21, author's italics).

Some people, perhaps most people, perceive church unity in terms of happiness and confidence in leaders. But it is deeper than that. It is unity of purpose—common commitment to a task that causes us to lay aside personal preferences for the sake of our main mission.

To have unity we don't have to agree on every issue. We don't have to like everything about the preacher. We don't have to be happy with every program, but we do have to work together and not let those minor differences divert us from our major purpose.

In the sermons that follow we will look at the causes and the cures of church conflict. And we will explore ways we can achieve peace and unity so *the world might believe.*

—*Paul W. Powell*
Dallas, Texas

1
The Church in Travail

In Gore Vidal's *Lincoln*, President Lincoln's oldest son, Bob, wanted to join the army and fight for the Union. His mother objected strenuously, and his father supported her decision. They had already lost two sons at an early age, and she could not bear the thought of losing another. Robert protested that soon General Burnside would be marching against Fredericksburg and would take Richmond by Christmas. Then the war would be over. His father replied, "Oh, no! No, boy, there will be war enough to go around."

It is with conflict as it is with war—there is always enough to go around, even among God's people. Just look at biblical history. Adam and Eve were scarcely settled in their new home in the suburbs of Eden when there arose conflict between their two sons and Cain killed his brother, Abel. Thereafter the pages of the Old Testament are darkened by conflict between the herdsmen of Abraham and his nephew, Lot; Jacob and his brother, Esau; Joseph and his brothers; David and Saul; and on and on.

In the New Testament the picture is no better. As Jesus moves progressively toward Jerusalem where He will eventually die on the cross, His disciples dispute among themselves as to who will be greatest in the kingdom. The New Testament church was still reeling from the effects of Pentecost when there arose a "murmuring" (Acts 6:1) among the Greek widows that threatened the unity and fellowship of the church.

The enthusiasm and optimism of the church's first great missionary effort was soon blunted by conflict over doctrine. It took the Jerusalem conference on salvation to settle the issue and send the missionaries out once again.

Even the first missionaries, Paul and Barnabas, had a "sharp contention" over missionary personnel and procedures—so strong, in fact, that it resulted in a split in their missionary endeavors (see Acts 15:39).

Those kinds of conflict are still going on in the church today. While returning from a meeting of our denomination years ago, I sat next to the late Dr. Ramsey Pollard, successor to Dr. R. G. Lee at the Bellevue Baptist Church, Memphis, Tennessee. As Dr. Pollard and I talked about his long and eventful ministry he wearily observed, "Paul, after forty-seven years in the ministry, it is harder to be pastor of a church today than at any time I have ever known."

Evidence everywhere confirms Pollard's statement. In a single eighteen-month period of 1989-90, over 2,100 Southern Baptist ministers were terminated. (Results of a survey conducted by Norris Smith of the Research Department, The Sunday School Board of the Southern Baptist Convention). I can only speak for my denomination. When you realize that there are approximately 39,000 Southern Baptist churches, that means that one out of every nineteen ministers was fired in a year and a half. That's 117 a month, twenty-eight a week, four a day. And, both the number and the percentage are growing each year.[1]

The reasons given run the gamut:

- There is difficulty in pleasing both the "old guard" and younger members. The pastor often finds himself in the midst of generational polarities over which he normally has little control.
- The congregation may feel the church is not growing as fast as it should, no matter how hard the pastor might be working.
- There is often poor communication between the pastor and laypersons on congregational life and goals.
- Some pastors demonstrate an excessive authoritarian approach to leadership. (Occasionally his problem is the opposite; he has practically no authority and leadership.)
- Pastoral misconduct is discovered (different kinds of moral turpitude).

THE CHURCH IN TRAVAIL

Another survey (based on responses from 220 missions directors throughout our denomination) also reported that:

- The highest number of forced terminations occurred in churches with fewer than 300 members,
- Many pastors are fired a second time at a different church.

While the figures state that 117 churches became fed up with their pastors each month of the year, you could probably multiply by ten the number of pastors who got fed up with their churches. In our denomination there are far more ordained persons out of the pastorate than in it!

Why are so many pastors leaving the ministry? The reasons are legion: lack of sufficient living expenses, insufficiency of privacy, general apathy ("malaise," as Jimmy Carter called it) of the congregation, and unreasonable expectations about how to make the church grow.

With so many pastors today either burned out, washed out, thrown out, or found out, and so many congregations either dead, declining, or divided, it is evident that the church today is a church in travail.

Just Looking at the Top of It

The more I know of our troubled churches the more I feel like the two rubes at the rail of a troop transport, gazing at the Atlantic for the first time.

"Man, look at all that water," said one. "Far as you can see in any direction. Nothing but water."

"Yeah, and that ain't all," said the other. "You are just looking at the top of it."

Most people have no clue as to the depth of the conflict that is taking place in many churches. We are just looking at the top of it.

Often this conflict in the church spills over into the minister's marriage and disrupts it also. At any one time the legal staff of the Annuity Board is dealing with more than 100 divorce cases as they relate to the division of a person's retirement income. These are pastors, church staff members, and institutional or agency employees; more than 200 every year. That's frightening, really frightening!

Conflict and the emotional debris it leaves behind is an inescapable part of life. We can never fully eliminate it. We can only hope to manage it and use it constructively.

Why So Much of It?

But, you ask, "Isn't love supposed to be the distinguishing mark of a believer? Aren't we commanded to live together in peace and unity? Why, then, is there so much conflict, especially in the church?" There are, I believe, several explanations.

First, it is due to our sinful nature. Even though the church is made up of people who have been redeemed and given a new nature in Christ, the old sinful nature is still in us and keeps asserting itself (Rom. 7:19-20).

The writer of James cuts to the heart of this issue when he asks, "From whence come wars and fightings [quarrels, disputes] among you?" Then he answers his own question, "Come they not hence, even of your lusts [desires] that war in your members?" (Jas. 4:1). Clearly, conflict has its roots in our sinful nature.

Larry McSwain wrote:

> Is conflict [in the church] necessary, then? Yes, because sin has made its impression upon all persons. Must it be so prevalent in the church? Yes, for the church is a community of sinners being saved by grace. It has not yet been redeemed in God's future kingdom.

Satan is the ultimate source of confusion and conflict as he appeals to our sinful nature. The apostle Paul urged believers to forgive one another and be reconciled to one another, "Lest Satan should get an advantage of us: for we are not ignorant of his devices" (2 Cor. 2:11). The word *device* in the Greek means "strategies" or "plans of attack." Satan uses divisiveness as one of his chief weapons.

Someone said, "Our tempers get us into trouble and our pride keeps us there." The Bible wastes no time pointing out the explosive power of anger. The first mortal man born in the world, Cain, in a jealous rage killed his brother.

And the first recorded conversation between procreated man and God was a warning against the destructive effects of anger. God told Cain that his anger was like a wild beast crouching at his door ready to devour him. Anger ultimately destroyed Cain and it will destroy us if it is not dealt with correctly.

Once we have become angry, our pride keeps us from admitting we are at fault, or forgiving those who hurt us. We get locked into positions and will not change. We become territorial, unreasonable, argumentative. We all have some of Cain's temper and pride in us and we must deal with them or they will destroy us and others.

Some conflict comes in the church because we have adopted the world's standards. Some churches look at their pastor as a chief executive officer. They hire him to produce and when he doesn't they fire him. There are some pastors who view themselves as a corporate executive with total authority over the congregation. They often wind up being their own worst enemy.

In 1990 the state of Texas had a hotly contested governor's race between oilman-rancher Clayton Williams and state treasurer Ann Richards.

Clayton Williams conducted the most expensive governor's race ever, spending $20 million—$8.5 million out of his own pocket.

From the beginning Williams had a substantial lead in all the polls. But, as the race progressed, he literally talked himself out of the governor's job. Through a series of self-destructive gaffes, Williams, a political novice, gave the victory to Ann Richards.

"His self-inflicted wounds bled him to death," noted a Republican consultant. "He just couldn't seem to keep his boot out of his mouth," commented another.

And Clayton Williams himself confessed, "I shot myself in the foot, then reloaded and shot myself again."

Pastors sometimes do the same thing by arrogant and self-serving attitudes.

Some conflict is due to our church polity. There is no hierarchy in our denomination. We believe in congregational rule. On a regular basis our churches have business conferences where the affairs of the church are supposed to be conducted in an open, democratic forum. Ideally, in such meetings anyone can stand up and say what they think—even if they don't think.

Since people do not hold the same convictions, share the same values, or see things the same way, we often have honest differences. And since people can be cruel and blunt in how they express themselves, these meetings often lead to conflict.

At such times words can become weapons. Alan Redpath, in his book, *A Passion for Preaching*, says he once formed a mutual encouragement fellowship in a time of stress in one of his pastorates. The members subscribed to a simple formula applied before speaking of any person or subject that was perhaps controversial.

T—is it true?
H—is it helpful?
I—is it inspiring?
N—is it necessary?
K—is it kind?

If what they were about to say did not pass those tests, they promised to keep their mouths shut! And it worked! It would help if we had such an agreement in our churches today.

Sometimes conflict ensues because we are resistant to change. Most of us have a personal "comfort zone," and we resist change because it involves too many risks and too much energy—but a healthy church is always changing, and conflict and change go hand in hand. Change begets conflict; conflict begets change.

And some conflict is due to the times in which we live. I spoke with a school superintendent recently who had just been fired. He shared that of the 1,050 school districts in Texas, 105 superintendents had been fired in the first six months of the school year. And, if predictions hold up, a total of 400 would be fired by the end of the school year.

Such conflict in our schools is but an expression of the anger and hostility in society as a whole. Newspapers and television carry daily reports of increased violence in our society—crime, alcoholism, divorce, drug abuse. Conflict in one area of our life will soon affect all our relationships. It is inevitable, then, that conflict in society will soon spill over into the church.

All of this makes me feel like Eugene Ledbetter. He and Jerry Clower, so Jerry tells, went coon hunting. They treed a coon but could not budge him from the tree. So, Eugene decided he'd climb the tree and shake the coon loose. But, to his surprise, it was not a coon up the tree. It was a wildcat. In a little while Jerry heard the "awfullest" commotion up in the tree you could imagine. Then came the voice of Eugene screaming, "Jerry! Jerry! Shoot up here amongst us. One of us has got to have some relief."

Everything Depends on It

With conflict so much a part of life, we must learn to handle it constructively. When I was being interviewed by the search committee of the Annuity Board of our denomination, one question asked was, "How do you handle conflict?"

That was an excellent question. Behind it was not only the realization that conflict is everywhere there are people, but that ultimately, our success in any endeavor will be in direct proportion to our ability to manage our differences and get along with other people.

A recent survey indicated the most common reason for being fired in secular employment was incompetence—39 percent. Incompatibility, the inability to get along with others, was second—17 percent. Then came dishonesty—12 percent; negative attitudes—10 percent; lack of motivation—7 percent; failure to follow instructions—7 percent; and other—8 percent.[2]

I don't know of any official studies, but my guess is, the same percentages would be true in the church. So our ability to relate to others, almost as much as our intellect, professional skill, experience or training, will ultimately determine our success in life.

John Wooden, the legendary basketball coach at UCLA, was one of the great coaches of all time. His teams won an unprecedented ten national championships in twelve years. Gayle Goodrich, one of his many star players at UCLA and later an all-pro with the Los Angeles Lakers, said of him, "Coach Wooden's greatest attribute was his ability to really understand people, to communicate with the players, and to bring them together as a team."

Understanding others, good communications, the ability to unite people; those are the keys to being a winner anywhere, anytime, and in any field.

An Unnatural Act

But, living together in peace is easier said than done. Relationships are so fragile. They can be broken by a single word or an innocent act. And, once broken they are hard to mend.

It takes forgiveness to heal broken relationships correctly and completely. And, forgiveness is never easy. It is achingly difficult. Long after you have forgiven, the wound lives on in memory.

Most of all, forgiveness is an unnatural act. It is against all instincts. What we really want when we are wronged or hurt is "an eye for an eye, and a tooth for a tooth" (Matt. 5:38).

Sigmund Freud understood this law of nature. "One must forgive one's enemies," he said, "but not before they have been hanged."

This creates an enormous problem for those of us called Christians, for our faith is shot through with forgiveness. But, in spite of the problem, in spite of the difficulty, we can forgive and we can live together in peace.

Jesus taught us to pray, "Forgive us our [trespasses], as we forgive [those who trespass against us]" (Matt. 6:12) At the center of this prayer, which Jesus gave as a model of how we ought to pray, lies the fact that we are no longer to live on the level of our natural instincts. We, through Christ, have a higher nature and by yielding to it can live our lives on a higher plane.

By His grace, the fruit of the Spirit—"love, joy, peace, longsuffering, gentleness, goodness, faith, Meekness, temperance"—can characterize our lives (Gal. 5:22).

Then, and only then, will we quell the travail in the church and live together in peace.

Notes

1. Larry McSwain and William C. Treadwell, *Conflict Ministry in the Church* (Nashville: Broadman Press, 1981), 24.
2. Robert Half Organization, reported in *The Dallas Morning News.*

2
The Conflict Within

The headlines read "Tyson vs. Tyson." It was a 1987 newspaper article about Mike Tyson, once the heavyweight boxing champion of the world. Two years earlier Tyson, at the age of 21, had become the youngest man in history to hold that title.

When I first preached this Tyson had won all thirty-seven of his professional fights, thirty-three of them by knockouts, and eighteen of them in the first round. And with at least ten good years before him, most people who knew boxing believed Tyson could dominate boxing as no other fighter before him.

But, according to Jose Torres, a longtime friend, Tyson was beset with so many problems in his personal life that he was a "walking time bomb."

A product of Brooklyn's toughest neighborhood, he spent time in his early life in several detention centers. According to Torres, he was a street brawler, a reckless driver, a heavy drinker, and a womanizer who boasted of his conquest over women, both sexually and physically but, who, at the same time, had a strong dependence on others.

Then Torres, citing Tyson's stormy personal life, made an interesting observation: "The man who will beat Tyson isn't a top-ten contender. It isn't Evander Holyfield or Ray Mercer, or even George Foreman. The man who will beat Mike Tyson is Mike Tyson." Then he added, "The only real challenge in sight for Tyson is his fight within." Sure enough, Torres was right. At the height of his career, in February 1990, Tyson was knocked out by an unheard-of Buster Douglas. A victim, by his own admission, of too much alcohol and too many women.

Tyson is back. As this book goes to the typesetter, Tyson is in hot water again. After a highly publicized trial in Indianapolis, Tyson has been convicted of raping a Miss Black America contestant.

While on vacation recently I watched the Academy-Award-winning movie *Platoon*. It was about the United States's involvement in the Vietnam War. It depicted not only the cruel and inhumane way some of our soldiers treated the enemy, but also how brutally they treated one another.

In the closing scene, one of the American soldiers who survived the war was reflecting on his experiences in Vietnam, and he said, "I think now, as I look back, we didn't fight the enemy, we fought ourselves. The real enemy was within us."

Isn't that how it most often is? The greatest enemy we have is ourselves, and the biggest battles we fight are within.

Any realistic dealing with conflict must begin with ourselves. For as Dag Hammarskjold, former general secretary of the United Nations, observed, "A man at war with himself will be at war with everyone else."

If we are to live together in peace and harmony in our churches we must first be at peace with ourselves. Otherwise we may allow our inner conflicts to spill over into our other relationships.

The apostle Paul was experiencing some of these inner conflicts when he wrote, "For, when we were come into Macedonia, our flesh had no rest, but we were troubled on every side; without were fightings, within were fears" (2 Cor. 7:5).

Paul was there giving a report on his missionary movements and emotions. He had been in Troas. From there he had sent Titus to Corinth with a strongly worded letter to that troubled church. In time, Paul grew restless waiting for Titus to return with a situation report. Would the church at Corinth receive him and repent, or would they reject Paul and his message? Would his work in Corinth be in vain? How would the church he loved respond?

Anxious, worried, afraid, he decided to cross the Aegean Sea into Macedonia to meet Titus as he returned. In these verses he tells us what happened when he arrived there.

He found no rest, no relaxation, no relief from either outward strife or inward stress. "We were," he said, "troubled on every side." Everywhere Paul turned he faced constant, straining, exhausting pressure. He summed up his situation by saying, "Without were fightings, within were fears."

In these words Paul tells us he actually fought battles on two fronts: one was on the outside and the other on the inside. One was external and the other, internal. He struggled outwardly with his enemies and inwardly with his emotions. Without there were fightings—wranglings, strifes, persecutions. Within there were fears, battles he fought within himself.

I can identify with that, can't you? While we all face some opposition from without occasionally, our biggest battles are within. There are not many people out to get us. Only occasionally is there someone who wants to hurt us, fire us, run us off. As Bill O'Brien put it, "The greatest indictment against Christians today is that no one wants to crucify us." But inwardly, we do continually battle with our emotions.

The word translated "fears" is the Greek word for "phobias" *(phobos)*. It suggests the idea of alarm, terror, and anxiety. Was Paul afraid? Yes! He was a human being, and to be human is to experience fears. The difference among people is not that some are afraid and others are not. The difference is that some are mastered by their fears and others are not.

What was Paul afraid of? Perhaps of bodily harm. To be a missionary in the first-century world (and even now) was to be engaged in hazardous work. Perhaps he was afraid of failure—that his work in Corinth had been in vain. Paul seemed to have been haunted by the fear that he had run in vain or that he would have labored in vain. Perhaps he was afraid of rejection, that his hard-hitting letter to the Corinthian church had been too severe and it might cause them to reject him. We cannot be exactly sure of what Paul was afraid of. We can only know he was afraid for he told us so.

There are all sorts of emotions and feelings that well up within us. We struggle with pride and passion, with anger and anxiety, with doubt and depression, with envy and inferiority. But of all these emotions, fear, I believe, is the most common and the most destructive. If we could just make our lives off-limits to fear, many of our illnesses would vanish. And we would live happier and healthier lives.

Fear has many faces. At times it wears the face of danger. At times it wears the face of rejection. At times it wears the face of failure or inadequacy. And at times it wears the face of insignificance.

What are the greatest fears that confront ministers today? There are four that I believe haunt every servant of God.

You Don't Have to Be Remarkable

The first fear we face is the fear of failure. This is a fear that grips almost everyone, even the most successful and the seemingly secure.

You might think that highly successful people are not afraid of failure anymore. But the opposite is true. The more successful a person is the more he has to lose. The higher he climbs, the further he has to fall. And the more people there are watching him.

So, no matter what a person has achieved, how successful they have been, they still struggle with this fear. This truth came home to me one day when on a flight to a speaking engagement I picked up an airline magazine that featured an article on successful corporate executives. One of them, talking about his emotions, said, "Occasionally when I am flying the thought flashes through my mind, *I wish this plane would go down and I would be killed while I am still on top of my business.*"

When I was struggling with giving up the pastorate to become leader of the Annuity Board of the Southern Baptist Convention I listed what I would give up and what I would gain in two columns side by side on a piece of paper. Do you know what one of the reasons I listed for going was? It was that it gave me a chance to leave while I was still on top.

I had been at my present position seventeen years. We had met with every success imaginable. Yet I knew I could still fail. Like that business executive, I know, and we all know, it is easier to climb to the top than to stay on top. And as the old psychiatrist said to a group of pastors, "It is never too late to fail." We are never beyond temptation. A runner can stumble on the last lap of the race. That's why the fear of failure is always there.

Winston Churchill was voted the most influential man of the first half of the twentieth century, but his son Randolph said, "I constantly had to reassure my father that his life had not been a failure."

How do we deal with the fear of failure? In Dr. Daniel Levinson's book, *In Seasons of a Man's Life,* he wrote, "When a man no longer feels he must be remarkable, he is more free to be himself and work according to his own wishes and talents."

It helps to remember what Somerset Maugham said, "Only the mediocre are always at their best." Have you discovered yet that you don't have to be remarkable, that God does not compare us to others, that you can fail at times without being a failure, and that failure doesn't have to be final? Knowing those things sets us free to struggle to be *our* best, not necessarily *the* best.

So, like Paul, we can say, "Without [are] fightings, within [are] fears." And one of the biggest fears we face is the fear of failure.

Giving a Body Slam to the Body of Christ

A second fear almost all of us face is the fear of rejection. The ultimate rejection, of course, is termination. We will deal with that specifically later, but the most common and one of the most devastating forms of rejection is criticism. While I am fairly secure, and while I know criticism comes to all who are in the public eye, and while I know it doesn't take much size to criticize, I want you to know it still eats my guts out.

Like you, I not only want to be successful, I also want to be liked, loved, and appreciated. There is a little of Teddy Roosevelt in most of us. His son once said of him, "Father always wanted to be the bride at every wedding and the corpse at every funeral." Don't we all?

And the thing that gets me most about church work is that people can be so petty in their criticism. Mike Yaconelli in *The Wittenburg Door* (Dec. 1984-Jan. 1985) wrote, "The problem with the church today is not corruption. It is not institutionalism. No, the problem is far more serious than something like the minister running away with the organist. The problem is pet鱼ness. Blatant petﾐness."

Henry M. Stanley was commissioned by a New York newspaper to go to Africa in search of Dr. David Livingstone. When Stanley returned to New York, after finding Livingstone, his newspaper gave him a banquet, to which many celebrities were invited. A young newspaperman asked Stanley if he was bothered by lions, elephants, or crocodiles. Mr. Stanley said, "No, young man, I stayed away from the lions and the crocodiles." Then the newspaperman said, "Didn't anything bother you while you were in Africa?" Then Stanley replied, "Yes, young man, if you must know the truth, I was almost eaten alive by the pesky chiggers."

It has been the same with me in the church. It has not been the lions or the elephants that have bothered me. It has been those blasted, pesky church chiggers with their nagging, petty criticism that have caused me the most trouble. They have irritated me no end.

Pettiness, of course, is not limited to the church. Other people have to contend with it, too. John Wooden, as you are now aware, was one of my coaching heroes. He coached UCLA successfully year after year, setting tremendous records. And, most remarkable of all, he did it during the turbulent years from 1964 until 1975. After seven championships in a row, Wooden's team lost in 1974. The next year they regained the national championship. On the floor of the San Diego Sports Arena, in 1975, after Wooden had won his last NCAA title, a booster sought him out and exulted, "Great victory, John. It made up for you letting us down last year." Can you believe that? But that's the way people can be about anything.

The long-range plans committee of my last full-time church conducted a survey among our members to find out what they thought about the location, program structure, and leadership of our church. We were trying to discover what they thought our potential for growth was, their willingness to make a financial commitment to a building program. So they distributed a church membership questionnaire to our people through the Sunday School. There were specific questions, most of them multiple choice, and then space was left at the end for the people to write additional comments they wanted to make. They were then to return the questionnaire unsigned.

I can't believe a person as smart as I am would agree to that, but I did. One of the questions we asked on the survey was, "How large can our church become?" It was a multiple-choice question with three choices:

A. As large as God wants us to be.
B. We are big enough.
C. We should concentrate on starting new churches.

Somebody crossed out "God" and added "King Paul" for their answer.

Our church had fifteen staff members, eight mission pastors, and a total of ninety-two people on our payroll. Yet, one of our members wrote on their survey, "I feel that we have finally become large enough to let each minister direct his area without any strings." How ridiculous. That's like saying a professional football team should be able to play without a quarterback or a huddle.

In the visitor's packets we distributed to our guests each Sunday we had a white stick-on name tag for them to sign and place on their garment. When I greeted the visitors I usually said something like, "Please put your name on the white name tag and stick it on your lapel so our people will recognize you as a visitor." One of our people wrote: "Ask the pastor if he would remember that women visit too and don't have lapels." By that time I had read hundreds of surveys, and I wanted to ask that person, "Why don't you stick it in your ear?"

When I read those comments, it caused me to recall a statement read years ago: "The difference between genius and stupidity is that genius has its limits."

They made me feel like A. J. Gordon when he was being interviewed by the pulpit committee of a large church in Boston. The questioning went on for hours. Finally one man asked, "Brother Gordon, would you be willing to go to hell for the glory of God?" Brother Gordon answered, "No, but I'd be willing for this committee to do so."

Let me give you some good counsel—don't ever conduct a survey like that. When you do, you invite every crackpot to take a potshot at you—anonymously. Or, as our assistant minister of music, Todd Wilson, put it, "You invite people to give a body slam to the body of Christ." You don't have to invite criticism. Plenty of it will come unbidden.

We received over 1,500 surveys back from our people. Not more than two dozen were critical of anything. The rest were supportive, encouraging, and upbuilding. But those few negative ones hurt—and we had asked for them. But of all the surveys returned that lady's on the name tags was the only one that spoke a word about the way we greeted visitors. But I promise you, thereafter I never greeted visitors or talked about those name tags but that criticism came to my mind. It was caught there like a fishhook. Isn't it amazing how we can overlook all the positive aspects and focus on the negatives in life? It's a part of our insecurity.

Criticism and the feeling of rejection that comes with it is inevitable. It is no respecter. The Israelites criticized Moses for taking too much on himself (Num. 16:13). The Pharisees criticized Jesus as being "beside Himself." And the Judaizers criticized the apostle Paul for promoting himself (Gal. 1:10).

Your success in the ministry will ultimately depend on how you deal with criticism, so don't act or react in haste. One of Lawrence Peter's less-famous principles goes like this: "Speak when you are angry, and you will make the best speech you will ever regret."

Paul's advice is solid, "Be ye angry and sin not: let not the sun go down upon your wrath. Neither give place to the devil" (Eph. 4:26-27). When I am especially angry, I usually sit down and write a scalding letter to the person I am mad at. I leave it on my desk overnight and then throw it away the next day. I vent my frustration without hurting anyone or doing more damage. And, almost any problem looks different in twenty-four hours.

A Basket Case or a Casket Case

Third, the fear we face is the fear of inadequacy. This is the fear of not measuring up, of being in over our heads, beyond our capacities. It is the fear that we simply cannot meet the demands or measure up to the expectations of people.

A study of the United Church of Christ indicated that the number-one reason clergymen left the pastoral ministry was a sense of personal and professional inadequacy. (G. Jud E. Mills and G. Burch, ex-pastor, *Why Men Leave the Ministry,* Philadelphia: Pilgrim Press, 1970.)

The congregation I pastored had over 7,500 members. On a given Sunday there were people in church from age five to ninety-five. There were children, young people, young married, middle-aged, and senior citizens.

There were zealots and Laodiceans, far-outs and far-ins, rich and poor, Ph.D.'s and high-school dropouts, ex-cops and ex-cons, active people who wanted to change everything and others who said, "We've-never-done-it-that-way-before." And they were all expecting something different from the pastor. In times of crisis they often felt betrayed because I didn't meet their needs or their expectations. And when human needs go unmet, conflict arises. In fact, you may have ministered to and met the needs of a person a dozen times, but fail them just once and they will most often be unhappy with you.

And, beyond that, there were so many demands on my time that I couldn't possibly meet them all. There was always someone dying, always someone divorcing, always someone depressed, always someone disappointed, and they all wanted to see me—right then. I think I know how Jesus felt when His disciples said to Him, "[Master,] all men seek for thee" (Mark 1:37). I felt like the man who had an identity crisis and an energy crisis at the same time. He didn't know who he was, and he was too tired to find out. The Old Testament prophet, Jonah, was swallowed by a whale but the modern prophet is likely to be nibbled to death by a thousand minnows. All of this produces enormous pressure and stress.

Psychologist Joan Broysenko is an expert on stress, associated with the Harvard Medical School. She insists that a high percentage of our physical illnesses are caused by stress or are stress related. Some gastro-intestinal disorders, some skin disorders, and the general weakening of our immune system have been traced to stress. And, she has concluded that fear is the core condition with all stress. Think about it for a minute. Stress arises out of fear of failure, fear of ridicule, fear of not measuring up, fear of being fired, fear of not making the next promotion, fear of not getting called to the next church, fear of having one day be just as boring as the day before. These are just a few of the fears that can drive us ordinary people to distraction.

We must learn to deal with the pressures and the stress of these multitudinous demands on us, or we will become either a basket case or a casket case.

How can we do this? The answer is found in the words of Paul that were inscribed on a plaque presented to me by the Alabama State Convention on the occasion of my installation as president of the Annuity Board: "Who then is capable for such a task? We are not like so many others who handle God's message as if it were cheap merchandise; but because God has sent us, we speak with sincerity in his presence, as servants of Christ" (2 Cor. 2:16b-17, GNB).

No Way to Make a Living

The fourth fear we face is the fear of termination. Based on statistics, obviously, the fear of termination is justified.

Then when you consider those churches that would like to fire their pastors and have not figured out how to do it as yet, or those who would like to but are too kind, perhaps it should be intensified. At the least it means our churches are troubled.

For a man to volunteer for the ministry today is to volunteer for hazardous duty. Being a pastor today is like being called on to play goalie on a hockey team without shin guards or a face mask.

You may be thinking, *That's the least of my fears. That could never happen to me.* Let me remind you that merely because you are not paranoid is no sign people are not out to get you.

Though I had been pastor at Green Acres Baptist Church for seventeen years, I still experienced this fear. When I heard of people who were critical of me, a feeling of insecurity and fear almost always came to me initially. Rationally, I knew they could never fire me. After all those years I had performed too many weddings of their daughters. I had buried too many of their relatives. I had baptized too many of their children. Rationally I knew it, but emotionally I felt it and feared it.

When I think of all that a pastor goes through I sometimes feel like the late A. Bartlett Giammetti president of the National (baseball) League and former president of Yale University. He began his book with this statement, "Being President of a university is no way for an adult man to make a living."

I recently visited with an associational director of missions who has spent twenty years working with churches and pastors. He noted more pastors leave the ministry due to personal problems than church problems; more churches are victimized by pastors than vice versa. If he is right, the first cause of concern and conflict must be ourselves.

Where can we find help for the fears within as well as the fightings without? Paul gives us the answer, "Nevertheless, God that comforteth those that are cast down, comforted us by the coming of Titus" (2 Cor. 7:6). The word *comfort* is the Greek word *parakleo* that means "to come beside." Paul was saying that in his hour of need the Lord came beside him, strengthened, and sustained him. That is always the case. When the disciples were

THE CONFLICT WITHIN

caught in the storm crossing the Sea of Galilee our Lord came alongside them. When the disciples walked along the road to Emmaus following Jesus' crucifixion and resurrection, wringing their hands in hopelessness, their hearts already having been wrung, the Lord came alongside them. When Paul was on trial before the Roman court, and all his friends had deserted him, the Lord came alongside him and strengthened him. In the same manner, He is always coming to us, giving Himself to us, and strengthening us for the conflicts without and within. In the final analysis, He is all we have, and He is all we really need.

How does God comfort us? How does He come to us? He came to Paul through Titus. He may come to us in the same manner, through a friend or through a fellow worker, but it is His coming nonetheless. And that is the secret to victory over both the fightings without and the fears within.

Before I close this chapter let me reiterate that the bottom line of my thirty-five years as a pastor was overwhelmingly positive. It was a fantastic journey. In spite of the fightings and the fears there were fun and fruit and friends and fulfillment. I said to my last congregation the day I preached my final pastoral sermon, "I leave with no regrets and no bad memories. Sure, there have been conflicts and struggles, but they were minor compared to the joy I have found. And I can truthfully say, if I had a thousand lives to live I would want to be a pastor in all of them." Amen! And amen!

3
Obstacles to Taking the Promised Land

When Ronald Reagan succeeded Edmund G. Brown as governor of California in 1967, Brown gave this advice to Reagan: "There is a passage in *War and Peace* that every new governor with a big majority should tack on his office wall. In it Count Rostov, after weeks as the toast of elegant farewell parties, gallops off on his first cavalry charge and finds real bullets snapping at his ears. 'Why, they are shooting at me,' he says, 'Me, whom everyone loves!'"

You might as well know up front, the man out front, whether he is leading a cavalry charge or a Christian church is going to get shot at. Perhaps that's why Snoopy, in the comic strip "Peanuts," said, "I hate being head beagle." Conflict and criticism are a part of the leadership package—no matter who the head beagle is.

Moses' life illustrates what I am talking about. He was, without a doubt, one of the great leaders of all time. He took Israel, a nation of disorganized and demoralized slaves, and led them from Egyptian bondage, toward the promised land for forty years.

In Egypt their taskmasters had afflicted them with heavy burdens and made their lives bitter. They had been forced to serve Pharaoh with "rigor" (Ex. 1:13-14). The word "rigor" means "to break apart." They were forced to serve under the kind of cruel circumstances that not only break a person's back but also his spirit. Slavery by its very nature crushes people's hopes and stifles their initiative. So Israel became angry, bitter, and rebellious. Moses took these people, perhaps 2 million in number, and

OBSTACLES TO TAKING THE PROMISED LAND

led them for forty years as God molded them into a nation that would eventually give birth to His Son and our Savior, Jesus Christ.

Moses had all the qualities of a good leader.

- He had a vision—a clear sense of mission. He knew where he was going.
- He had courage—the faith to try, to risk.
- He had the determination to stick. When hardships and obstacles came his way, he did not waver, he persisted.
- He had a humble spirit. He was open to the advice of others and constantly sought the counsel of God.
- He did not try to do everything himself. He knew how to delegate and readily shared his responsibilities with others.
- He had a servant's heart. In fact, nowhere in Scripture does the Lord ever refer to him as "Moses, my leader." It was always, "Moses, my servant."
- He always had the best interest of his people at heart. At least five times, when the judgment came on Israel because of her sin, Moses pleaded with God in her behalf. If necessary, he prayed that God would blot his name out of the book He had written so the people could be forgiven.
- And Moses was a man of impeccable integrity.

Yet, Moses lived in constant conflict and with bitter, cutting criticism. At least twelve times the biblical record tells us of Moses in conflict because of his leadership.

Somebody has said a good leader is doing his job when half the people are following him and half are chasing him. That's the way it was with Moses most of the time.

The people criticized Moses about everything. They criticized him about his provision. When they ran low on water they accused him of bringing them into the desert to die of thirst.

When food became scarce they accused him of bringing them into the desert to starve to death. When God provided manna from heaven they soon grew tired of eating the same thing every meal and complained that they wanted a more varied diet.

They criticized Moses about his wife. After Zipporah, his first wife died, Moses married an Ethiopian woman. Aaron and

Miriam didn't like his marrying a foreigner and openly let their feelings be known. Leaders live in glass houses. Not only are they subject to criticism, so are their families.

They criticized Moses' leadership style. They said he took too much authority on himself. He didn't give the people enough say in making decisions. They felt he was overstepping his bounds as a leader.

And they criticized his plan for taking the promised land. When Israel reached the borders of Canaan and Moses urged them to possess it, they resisted and turned back into the wilderness where they wandered for forty years.

At times, Moses grew so weary of their complaints and the continual conflict that he cried to God for relief. He told the Lord he could not bear up under the load any longer.

What Moses faced, all leaders face. That's partly because leaders are change agents and people are generally resistant to change. As management consultant Roy Bletze said, "The only person who likes change is a wet baby." And sometimes, as you know, they don't even like it. You have to change them while they are kicking and screaming.

At times people resist change because they have no faith. They are afraid to risk, to launch out. At other times it is because they have honest differences. And still at times it is because they are just plain cantankerous.

But the fact is, the problems Moses faced and the kinds of people he had conflicts with exist in every age. And if you are going to be a leader, you need to accept that.

There were four groups in particular that Moses was in conflict with as he led the children of Israel for forty years. Those four kinds of people are still with us today.

Watch the Comfort Zone

The first group of people Moses had to contend with was the "back to Egypt committee" (see Ex. 14:10-14). This committee was formed before Israel got out of Egypt and became a standing committee. Every time the children of Israel encountered a problem or faced a danger the "back to Egypt committee" promptly met and said, "Moses, we told you so. We had things much better in Egypt, and we were foolish for leaving. Let's pack up and go back to Egypt."

The "back to Egypt committee" had its first meeting while Israel was encamped at Pihahiroth, on the Egyptian side of the Red Sea. Pharaoh, who had set Israel free because of the ten plagues, changed his mind and pursued them with 600 chariots and horsemen. As the Pharaoh's army approached, the children of Israel were "sore afraid" (v. 10) and they cried to the Lord. Then they began to complain that they should never have listened to Moses in the first place. They would have been better off to live as slaves than to die as free men. They were the first exponents of the "better red than dead" philosophy.

They quickly forgot the bitter servitude of Egypt and the cruel treatment of their taskmasters and talked only of returning to the security they had once known.

The "back to Egypt committee" was made up of fearful and faithless people who were afraid to risk. They were afraid of Pharaoh's army, afraid of the desert, afraid of the inhabitants of Canaan. Their motto was, "Nothing ventured, nothing lost." Forget the prospects of the promised land. Forget the hopes of a new life. They preferred the security of slavery to the risk of freedom.

Every church has its "back to Egypt committee," people who are fearful and faithless. People who are afraid to risk.

Charles Garfield has studied 1,500 outstanding achievers in nearly every walk of life. He found they all have certain traits in common—traits that are not innate, but which can be learned by everyone. One of them is "be willing to risk." Most people stay in what Garfield calls "The comfort zone"—settling for security, even if it means mediocrity and boredom, rather than taking chances.

The Tartar tribes of Central Asia used to have a curse they hurled against their enemies. They did not say to them, "Go to . . ." They said, "May you stay in one place forever." That is a horrible wish for anyone. Can you think of a worse fate to endure? To never change? To never progress? To never advance?

One of the challenges of leadership is to get people out of their comfort zone. It is to bolster their courage to trust God and make a run for new frontiers. So, Moses said to them, "Fear ye not, stand still, and see the salvation of the Lord, which he will show to you this day... The Lord shall fight for you" (Ex. 14:13-14). He tried to get them to take their eyes off the obstacles and see the Omnipotent. Such leadership will invariably lead to conflict, but it is the only way ever to get people to possess Canaan. And I remind you there has never been a statue erected to the memory of someone who was willing to let well enough alone.

Crybaby Christians

The second group Moses had to contend with were the "onion-and-garlic people" (Num. 11:11-12). Shortly after the children of Israel left Egypt the Lord began sending manna from heaven to feed them. Manna was a wafer-like bread with a honey flavor. When the children of Israel arose each morning God had rained fresh bread from heaven on them.

But it wasn't long until they were "fed up" with manna. Their theme song became, "It's manna in the morning, manna at the noontime, and manna when the sun goes down."

Perhaps they had eaten well in Egypt for they moaned, "We remember the fish, which we did eat in Egypt freely; the cucumbers, and the melons and the leeks, and the onions, and the garlic: But now our soul is dried away, there is nothing at all, besides this manna, before our eyes" (vv. 5-6).

Their complaining distressed Moses to no end. He went to the Lord in prayer and said, "Lord, have I conceived all this people? [Must I carry them to the promised land like a father carries a nursing child?]" (vv. 12).

The "onion-and-garlic people" are the immature saints, the

people who have never grown up, the crybabies who whine and complain anytime they don't get their way. I call them "onion-and-garlic people" because when you peel an onion you cry. When you eat garlic, the person you talk to cries.

I have dealt with my share of crybaby Christians in my thirty-five years as a pastor. In one of my early pastorates one of my staunchest supporters called one day very upset. Her husband, a postman by profession, had been off work on sick leave for a week and I had not visited him. When I asked what was wrong with him she said he had an infected ingrown toenail. When she said she was upset with me, I thought she was kidding and I laughed out loud. I said, "You are kidding, aren't you?" She wasn't! I was never taught in the seminary and I had never considered an infected ingrown toenail serious enough to necessitate a pastoral call, until then.

Once in a sermon I said, "There are no perfect marriages because there are no perfect people." At the close of the service a lady told me she resented that remark because, she said, her's was a perfect marriage.

In another sermon I quoted the words of Jesus, "Be ye therefore wise as serpents, and harmless as doves" (Matt. 10:16). Then I told the congregation that we have reversed that saying, and we are "as mean as snakes and as dumb as birds." That evening a member of the Audubon Society cornered me and ripped me up for insinuating that birds were dumb.

Years ago, as I was preparing to go to a new church field, I received several person-to-person, long-distance telephone calls when I was out of the office. The caller would never leave his name or number. Finally, he caught me in and when I answered the phone he asked me if I was moving to Tyler. When I answered, "Yes," he warned me to watch out for a certain man. He cautioned, "He's a vampire and he will eat your gut out." Needless to say, he had my attention.

I asked, "Who is this?" and the phone went "click!" He hung up on me.

Sure enough, I had not been in Tyler six months until I was in conflict with this man. I led our deacons to adopt a deacon standard policy. It was little more than a restatement of the qualifications of a deacon set out in 1 Timothy 3:8-13, with my Baptist interpretation (i.e., "He is to be a tither, a total abstainer from alcohol, etc."). And we added that if a deacon missed six monthly meetings in a row without an excused absence, he would be automatically dropped from the deacon body. It seemed reasonable to me, to our deacons, and to our church as a whole. So they approved the policy.

When a copy of this policy reached this deacon, who was a social drinker and who had not been to a deacons' meeting in over a year, he was incensed. He wrote me a threatening letter stressing, "I have seen churches split over less than this."

I promptly called him for lunch and discussed the matter. He accused me of kicking him off the deacon body. I assured him that neither I nor the church was kicking him off. If he was eliminated, it would be because he eliminated himself. All he had to do was comply with the church policy. I thought that settled the matter.

Fifteen years later he came to my study and broached the subject again. I reminded him of our earlier meeting and told him I thought we had resolved the issue at that time. When he insisted we had never dealt with it I reached into my files and pulled out the letter he had written to me fifteen years earlier. It is the only letter like that I had ever saved, and I saved it because of that anonymous phone call. I slid it across the desk to him and asked, "Whose signature is at the bottom of that letter?" He had to admit it was his. I had him dead to rights. So he jumped up and stalked out of the room in anger.

Can you imagine that? For fifteen years he had been sulking and pouting over the matter. When I discussed this with one of his close friends and fellow deacons, he said, "Don't pay any attention to him. He is a crybaby. He has been that way all of his life."

Vance Havner once observed, "The malady of the church today is infantile paralysis—too many babies who never grew up." I think he was right. Every leader must contend with the "onion-and-garlic people." There are carping, complaining crybabies everywhere.

Incidentally, speaking of onions, the late R. G. Lee was in great demand as a speaker throughout our nation. Following each evening speaking engagement, I am told, he would go to a cafe and order a glass of buttermilk and an onion sandwich. He would have the cook spread mayonnaise on two pieces of bread and then put big slices of onion between them to make the sandwich. He would then eat the sandwich and wash it down with the buttermilk.

When asked why he drank buttermilk and ate an onion sandwich every night, he replied, "The buttermilk helps me to sleep. The onion sandwich guarantees that I sleep by myself."

Hindsight, Foresight, and Insight

The third group Moses had to contend with was the "we-too-are-holy bunch" (see Num. 16:1-3). Korah, the great grandson of Levi, and 250 of the prominent leaders in Israel, rose up against Moses and said, "Ye take too much upon you, seeing all the congregation are holy, everyone of them, and the Lord is among them: wherefore then lift ye up yourselves above the congregation of the Lord?" (v. 3).

Korah and his followers resented Moses' leadership style. They thought he was too dictatorial, that he overstepped his bounds as a leader. He was not giving them enough say-so in the decision-making process.

Moses, of course, was not a dictator. The Bible says he was the meekest man who ever lived. The problem was not Moses. It was that these people did not understand and did not want good leadership. They wanted to be in charge. They wanted to run things themselves. They thought they knew better than Moses and God put together.

Every church has "we-too-are-holy" people in it. They are people who are ambitious and zealous for power. They don't understand good leadership and don't want leadership. Rather they resent it and resist it. They are constantly afraid the preacher is going to overstep his bounds and take too much authority on himself. They think they know better than the leader what ought to be done, and they want to be consulted on every decision.

There are plenty of people who don't understand leadership. Good leadership is not going to the people and saying, "We've got a problem. What do you think we should do about it?" Good leadership involves identifying the problem, finding the best solution, and then persuading people to follow your plan in solving it.

In Steinbeck's play, "The Moon Is Down," Mayor Orden is held prisoner by the enemy who brings cruel pressure upon him. Finally, his friend advises him to give up his resistance. He answered with the thrilling words, "They elected me not to be confused."

Leaders are people who are not supposed to be confused. They should know what the problems are, how to solve them, and be able to persuade other people to follow them in correcting the situation.

There are at least three leadership styles. There is leadership by *intimidation,* leadership by *manipulation,* and leadership by *inspiration.* Leadership by intimidation is leadership by fear. Leadership by manipulation is leadership by deceit. Leadership by inspiration is leadership by influence.

Leadership by influence is ultimately the only way for the pastor of a church to lead. And that kind of leadership must be earned. A few years ago a pastor I know moved to a new church. His first Sunday in the pulpit he showed a video clip from a well-known Christian leader appealing to the congregation to give their new pastor the "latitude to lead." The young man then proceeded to lay out his demands to his new congregation. As he listed demand after demand, one wise, elderly saint leaned over to her son and said, "He sure wants a lot on credit." Good leadership does not come on credit. You get it the old-fashioned way: You earn it.

How does Korah's remark, "We too are holy," fit in with our belief in the priesthood of the believer? We believe every Christian is holy. There is not a privileged, priestly class among God's people today as there was in Moses' day. Through Christ every believer has direct access to God. That's why we have a congregational church government. Some pastors are too dictatorial. They act as though they alone have a "hot line" to heaven.

But that does not minimize the need for strong leadership in our churches. In fact, most churches are floundering for lack of direction. Our churches need pastors who are not confused. They need leaders who see what needs to be done, who find a solution, and who challenge the people, "Come on, church, let's do it." If the people will not follow, we are not to try to force them. We are to honor the priesthood of every believer and respect the rule of the congregation. The fact is, they "too are holy."

The line between the priesthood of the believer, congregational rule, and good leadership is a thin line, but it can and must be walked.

There is an old Irish toast we need to remember: "May you have the hindsight to know where you've been, the foresight to know where you're going, and the insight to know when you're going too far." Wise is the leader who knows when he is going too far.

Grasshopper Christians/Grasshopper Churches

The fourth group Moses had to contend with were the "grasshopper-and-giant crowd." These were the pessimistic people who had no faith. Someone has defined a pessimist as a person who can look at the land of milk and honey and see only calories and cholesterol. Eighteen months out of Egypt, Israel came to the borders of the promised land. They had been in Egypt for over 400 years. God had miraculously freed them from captivity, and now they were at the border town of Kadesh-barnea. The promised land was theirs for the taking.

So Moses appointed a "Promised-land Search Committee" to spy out the land. The committee was composed of twelve members, one from each of the twelve tribes. Their mission was not to determine if they should take the promised land, but how. It was to bring word "by what way" they should go and into what cities they would come (Deut. 1:22).

After forty days they came back with a divided report. All twelve (100 percent) of them saw the same thing: rich fruits, great abundance, and giants. They even brought back clusters of grapes on a staff to prove that it was a land that flowed with abundance, milk and honey, but they were not agreed on the advisability of trying to take the land.

The perspective of the majority of the spies (83.33 percent) was negative. They focused on the superiority of the giants and the inferiority of the tribes. They said, "We saw the giants:... and we were in our own sight as grasshoppers, and so we were in their sight" (Num. 13:33). They overlooked the grapes and riveted their attention on the giants.

Only two (16.67 percent) of the spies saw the giants in proper perspective. Joshua and Caleb focused on their God-given mission of taking the promised land and said, "Let us go up at once, and possess it: for we are well able to overcome it" (v. 30). "If the Lord delight in us, then he will bring us into this land, and give us" (14:8).

What happened when the masses heard the two reports? The majority effectively transmitted their own feelings of inadequacy and pessimism. Negative thinking is always infectious. So the people concluded, "We [are] not able to go up against the people" (13:31).

Soon gloom and doom engulfed the whole camp. Pandemonium broke loose. They wept and wailed all night. They forgot everything but what they considered the great danger. They forgot the mercies of God and all His mighty dealings with them.

Rebellion followed. A movement was launched to impeach Moses and elect new leaders to take them back into the bondage of Egypt (Num. 14:1).

OBSTACLES TO TAKING THE PROMISED LAND

The problem with the "grasshopper-and-giant crowd" was that they saw the obstacles as greater than the opportunities. They focused on the giants instead of on God. Their fear was bigger than their faith. Their pessimism blinded them to the promises of God. They saw themselves as grasshoppers—thus they acted like grasshoppers.

Every leader must contend with the grasshopper-and-giant mentality. At every crossing of the road that leads to the future, each progressive spirit is opposed by a thousand pessimists appointed to guard the past. As someone has said, "Where there is a will—there is a won't."

We have a vast multitude of grasshopper Christians and grasshopper churches today. The late Danny Kaye said he once saw a sign in a vacant store window that read, "We undersold everybody, including ourselves." That's the danger we all face. Because of our lack of faith we will undersell ourselves and God.

The divine record tells us what happened to Israel. Everyone of them above twenty years of age fell in the wilderness, and only the two faithful spies entered the promised land forty years later. As God utterly discarded the cowardly Israelites, just so, from that day to this, He utterly discards people without faith and courage.

Never in the history of God's dealings with His people has He done anything with pessimists and cowards. People who think they can do nothing can do nothing because they cut themselves off from the source of strength. Man's unbelief limits the divine power. If a man has no faith, he will not try.

The challenge of leadership is to bolster the fledgling faith of people. It is to challenge them to see and seize the future. It is to inspire and motivate people to look beyond the giants to God, beyond doubt to faith, beyond their pessimism to the promises of God.

The poet put it this way,

> "Doubt sees the obstacles...
>   Faith sees the way:
> Doubt sees the darkest night...
>   Faith sees the day:

> Doubt dreads to take a step...
> Faith soars on high,
> Doubt questions... "Who believes?"
> Faith answers... "I."

Faith is the master builder. It has built every bridge across every chasm; every city on the wide-extended plains; every institution of learning whose doors are flung wide open to hungry minds; every church through whose gates of glory the worshipers come into its courts of praise.

The word of faith is, "All things are possible." The strong point of faith is that it connects itself with the power of God that can find no difficulties.

What are the lessons for leaders in Numbers 13? A few include:

- Only one in six people focuses on the possibilities. The other five focus on the problems.
- Gloom and doom may win that day, but they lose the future.
- When adults make cowardly decisions, children suffer for years.
- An unseized opportunity may not reappear until a new generation is raised up.
- We should never confuse the will of the majority with the will of God.
- Promised lands are not taken by majority vote but by the faith of a few daring people.
- Pushing the positive view may be hazardous to a leader's health (and safety).

The simple truth of this chapter is that conflict is a part of the leadership package—it always has been and always will be.

I think that's why Vance Havner said, "A preacher should have the mind of a scholar, the heart of a child, and the hide of a rhinoceros."

So don't be surprised or disheartened when conflict comes. Seize the moment and challenge the people to take the promised land before them. That's what leadership is all about.

Ultimately your success in life will depend on how you handle conflict, criticism, and opposition. By and large, Moses handled it as well as any man could, but in the end, in one instance, just one, he lost his cool and thus he lost his leadership. He was not permitted to take Israel into the promised land. A new leader, Joshua, did that.

One of the saddest scenes in all the Bible is that of a lonely, windswept mountaintop where Moses died all alone, unable to finish what God had called him to do—partly because he had not handled conflict and criticism correctly.

4
Working with the Power Structure of the Church

A pastor friend was on the verge of being fired by his church. As he tried to explain the situation to me, he told about a member of his church whose mother was a Christian but whose father was not. His mother was an angry, argumentative, combative kind of person, and so his parents had gone through a stormy marriage. One day after a heated family argument his father said to him, "Son, whatever you do, don't make the Christians mad." My friend then explained the trouble he was having in his church by saying, "Paul, that's my problem. I made the Christians mad."

We all know that Christians can get mad. And when they do they can be vicious. What may be nothing more than a barroom scrap, when it takes place in the church, has a way of escalating to the level of a holy war. In religious squabbles people tend to envision God as being on their side and eternal truth being at stake. So they fight "like heaven" for what they believe to be right. As the Texas proverb affirms, "There is no hatred like Christian hatred." No poison is as potent as the venom of the virtuous.

One of the major areas of conflict in many churches is with the power structure, that one or handful of people in almost every church, every organization, every community, who control the power, who run things, and without whose support and approval the church at large can hardly get anything accomplished. In the Epistle of 3 John there is a classic case of conflict with the power structure of the early church.

John wrote this epistle to commend Gaius, a prominent layman in the early church, for his support of traveling missionaries. In the infancy of the New Testament church, these itinerant preachers played a vital role in the spread of the gospel and the strengthening of the Christian fellowship. There were few trained leaders, and so these men traveled from place to place ministering to the congregations. It is probable that few preachers were wealthy enough to stand the expense of staying at inns. In any case, inns were notoriously wicked. It meant a great deal to the work of God for these men to be able to obtain food and lodging in the homes of fellow believers. Gaius was well known for showing such hospitality, and John commends him for it. He was a man with an open heart, an open hand, and an open house.

While he was writing to Gaius, John mentions another prominent member of the church, Diotrephes, who was of the opposite persuasion and with whom he was in conflict. John had written to the church earlier to encourage support of these missionaries, but Diotrephes had opposed him. He not only refused to assist the traveling missionaries himself, but at the threat of excommunication from the fellowship, he was forcing his views on the entire church. To accomplish his goals he was making hurtful statements about John and thus was creating conflict in the church.

John writes, concerning Diotrephes, "I wrote unto the church but Diotrephes, who loveth to have the preeminence among them, received us not. Wherefore, if I come, I will remember his deeds which he doeth, prating against us with malicious words and not content therewith; neither doth he himself receive the brethren, and forbiddeth them that would, and casteth them out of the church" (3 John 9-10).

This man Diotrephes is representative of the power structure, or perhaps better, the ringleader of the power structure that exists in many churches today. He was a strong-minded, aggressive, opinionated man who, by the sheer force of his personality, through family ties and friendships or through his place of leadership, had such a stranglehold on the church that he was stifling its missionary spirit.

Notice how John describes Diotrephes: "Who loveth to have

the preeminence among [the brethren]." The phrase "loveth to have the preeminence" literally means he was "fond of being first." Diotrephes was a little man with a big ego. He was possessive, domineering, opinionated, and malicious.

Notice what Diotrephes did: "[He] received us not." He opposed John's apostolic authority and sought to impose his own views on the rest of the church. Thus, he was disruptive and was creating conflict in the fellowship.

Notice the vehicle of his strife: "[he prateth] against us with malicious words." Diotrephes was spreading vicious, cutting, harmful gossip about John. His tongue was the vehicle of his strife. Words can be weapons. With them it is possible to assassinate the character of almost any good person and disrupt any fellowship.

Notice how John planned to deal with Diotrephes: "If I come, I will remember his deeds which he doeth." Literally, that means, "I will bring what he has done to his attention and to the attention of others." John intended to confront Diotrephes personally when he arrived. He was confident he would put him in his place on his next visit to the church.

The descendants of Diotrephes are still with us today. You will find at least one in almost every church. They are people who, by the strength of their personality, family ties and friendships, or the power of their influence, virtually run the church. Without their approval and support it is almost impossible to get anything done. They may not be vocal, visible, or vicious, but they are there and must be reckoned with.

They may be the chairman of the deacons (or elders, stewards, vestry, etc.) treasurer of the church, or head of the personnel committee. And in smaller churches they often receive the mail and pay all the bills.

They often want to be consulted on every issue, have a voice in every decision, and chair every committee. Many times they have a negative attitude and are known more for what they are against than what they are for.

They often resist leadership, insist on their own way, and enlist others to support their views. And, like Diotrephes, they invariably become a source of conflict in the church.

Perhaps you have noticed that the problems in most churches are not caused by big men wanting to serve, but by little men wanting to rule. It's usually the "little thinkers" who are the "big stinkers."

By the way, the word "preeminence" used here to describe Diotrephes is used only one other time in the New Testament. In Colossians 1:18 Paul writes concerning Christ, "That in all things *he* might have the preeminence" (author's italics). Christ is to be first in the church. And we are all to seek to do His will. When we seek the preeminence ourselves, when our will, whether we be pastor or layman, is put before God's will, conflict is sure to come.

Let it be clearly understood, any person who seeks to use the church as an arena for the display of one's personal power is an obstruction to the work of God. And such a person needs to be confronted.

How do we deal with the modern-day Diotrephes? How do we handle conflict in the church constructively? In the place where we serve, whether we are on staff or we serve as a layperson?

Let me share with you seven suggestions on how to minimize or come to grips with conflict with the power structure of the church.

Dragging Elephants

First, build a positive spirit in your church. Some pastors are known more for what they are against than what they are for. They are against shorts, against the Masonic lodge, against movies, against liberals, against almost anything and everything. They are negative, critical, caustic. If you are a loving, kind, supportive, and encouraging person, then in time you will likely develop a loving, kind, supportive, and encouraging congregation. If, on the other hand, you are a feisty, combative, do-or-die kind of person, you will likely develop that kind of spirit in your church fellowship. Fighting leaders produce fighting people. And loving leaders most often produce loving people.

At the height of the civil rights movement in the 1960s, George Wallace, governor of Alabama, was strongly opposed by some prominent businessmen in his own state. When asked why he opposed the governor, one man replied, "Wallace kept encouraging us, 'Stand up and fight! Stand up and fight!' So, we did. We stood up and fought him." If you are the kind of person who is always forcing "showdowns" and "shoot-outs," don't be surprised if one day you're the one shot down and shown the way out. If you are always encouraging your people to "stand up and fight," you can expect that one day they will stand up and fight you.

The best way to build an atmosphere of love and cooperation is to model a positive tone personally: by praising publicly the congregation's strengths; by enjoying and taking pride in the diversity among church members; by thanking critics, at least initially, for their candor and concern.

I have a pastor friend who is forever berating and scolding his people. He somehow manages in every service, either during his sermon, at announcement time, or just before the benediction, to rip them up for their lack of giving, witnessing, attendance, or friendliness. The result is that many of his people have either quit coming or, if they still attend, they leave church mad.

Somebody has said, "With a sweet tongue and kindness, you can drag an elephant by a hair." Love will always draw more and accomplish more than badgering and antagonism and laying guilt on people. So, build a loving spirit in your church. Focus on the joys of life rather than bemoaning discouragements. Don't dwell on your disappointments in people, failed programs, and lost votes. And, for sure, don't announce or denounce them from the pulpit.

Pullers Aren't Kickers

Two, keep your people busy. We have a saying in Texas, "A mule can't plow and kick at the same time." People who are involved in meaningful service for the Lord are less likely to be criticizing and kicking. Like any army, those on the front lines don't have time to complain. Griping is the luxury of those with small jobs or no jobs. Being in the battle isn't always fun or even desirable to those involved, but it certainly gives more satisfaction in Christian service and eliminates most strife. But make sure it is meaningful work, not just busy work. Keep them busy at the kinds of things Jesus talked about in Matthew 25: feeding, clothing, visiting, helping, befriending, loving, and witnessing. That's the real work of God. To fail to involve your people in real ministry is to turn committed Christians into frustrated critics.

A Towel, Not a Whip

Three, love and serve your people. In the closing days of His earthly ministry Jesus met with His disciples in the upper room (John 13). He had told them of His approaching passion, but they seemed oblivious to His words. As they chatted with one another Jesus poured water in a basin, wrapped a towel around His waist, and then moved throughout the group washing the feet of His disciples one by one. In so doing, Jesus was taking the role of a servant. In His day there were no concrete sidewalks or asphalt streets. And the only shoes people had were sandals. Naturally, when a person traveled from one place to another, his feet got dirty. And since they reclined on the floor with their feet up under them, rather than sitting in chairs as we do today, it was important that their feet be clean. So when guests arrived at a house for dinner, they were met at the door by a slave who washed their feet. That day, Jesus, the Lord of glory, stooped and washed His disciples' feet like a common servant. When He was through He said to them, "If I then, your Lord and Master, have washed your feet; ye also ought to wash one another's feet." Then He added, "I have given you an example that you should do [to one another] as I have done to you" (vv. 14-15).

This is the only time in Scripture that Jesus ever said, "I have given you an example." And it is when He took the role of a servant. We need to remember that the symbol of the pastor's office is a towel, not a whip.

Eric Sevareid said, "My observation about politics in many countries is that its practitioners fall into two categories. The boys who want positions in order *to be* something, and the men who want positions in order *to do* something." That is just as true of church politics as it is of governmental politics. If you love and serve your people they will know it and will likely love you in return. And when your people love and appreciate you, a few critics and cranks couldn't run you off if they wanted to.

I recently ran across this saying I have found to be true: "Love reduces friction to fraction." That's good. Really good!

Guess Who's Gone?

Four, respect your church's traditions. Every church has its own personality. They have certain customs and traditions that are important to them. When you go to a church, and especially when you are new on the field, it is your responsibility to learn what those traditions are and respect them. If you don't, conflict is sure to arise.

I once pastored a church that had the Lord's Supper table on the floor in front of the pulpit—probably just like your church has. But there was one difference. On each side of that Lord's Supper table was an empty chair. The table and chairs had been given as a memorial by a prominent family in that church and they had been there for years.

I pastored the church for five years and hardly noticed those two empty chairs. But they bothered a later pastor greatly. In fact, one Sunday he told the church that they reminded him of a riderless horse. He then moved them without asking anyone. The chairs had been there for years and they were important to that congregation. When he made an issue over them they felt he was attacking something sacred. Today the chairs are still there, and guess who is gone? That's what I mean by respecting the traditions of the church.

WORKING WITH THE POWER STRUCTURE OF THE CHURCH

Don't sacrifice your ministry over something as trivial as that. When challenged on issues by church members, some pastors react by retaliating or at least refusing on principle to compromise. Every issue is do or die with them. It's total victory, or perish gloriously in the attempt. To be that rigid is just not very smart. Fran Tarkenton in his book, *Playing to Win*, sounded a good warning when he said: "If you treat every situation as a life-and-death matter, you'll die a lot of times."

The older I have grown, the choosier I have become of my fights. I love the quote of Joseph Addison, "If I've got to be wounded, let it be by the paw of a lion and not the hoof of an ass." A bulldog can whip a skunk any day, but it is just not worth it. There are many battles that are just not worth fighting, even if you can win.

To be successful in church leadership you have to decide what is important and what's not. Then on matters of principle, stand like a rock; and on matters of preference, drift like a fog.

The late Senator Everett Dirksen once opined, "I am a man of principle, and my first principle is flexibility." That spirit helps in the church. It is especially important when you are new at a church.

At a recent convention I talked with a friend who is the minister of music for a church. He has a new pastor who has been on the field less than a year, so I asked how things were at the church. He said, "The new pastor is already in hot water." When I asked why, he replied, "He is trying to change too much too soon."

Lincoln once said, "I walk slow, but I never walk back." For the pastor it's almost always good policy to walk slow your first year in a church. After all, love "suffereth long, and is kind" (I Cor. 13:4). Being patient, calm, philosophical, and charitable will go a long way toward making a staff member loved and respected by his/her people.

So remember that your church has some traditions that are important to them. And while they may not mean much to you, they are important to them, and so they had better become important to you. Church traditions ought to be respected until you have earned the right to change them.

Call Me a Doctor

Five, be a friend to your people. Share outside interests with them as well as preach to them. You cannot sit in an ivory tower and know your people well. You must mix with them beyond the church. So play golf with them, fish or hunt with them, dine with them, visit in their homes—become their friend. When you are relaxed and at home with your people, you will have fewer conflicts.

I know of one pastor who said to his congregation his first Sunday on the field, "My wife and I will accept no social engagements our first year here." Well, they didn't have to worry about any invitations after that. The church tolerated him for several years, but they never loved him because they never knew him.

I was leading a Bible study in a church years ago. The first night in an effort to break the ice with the congregation, I gave them my usual spiel. "When I go to a new place people always want to know, 'What should we call you? Should we call you President Powell? Doctor Powell? Reverend Powell? Mister Powell? Or Brother Powell?'" Then after a brief pause, I quipped, "I really prefer to be called Saint Paul."

Everyone laughed except the pastor. After the Bible study was over and I turned the service back to him, he said to the congregation, "You may call him Paul if you like, but you call me Doctor."

Are you surprised to know that within a few months he was in trouble at his church? He was so formal and he kept himself so aloof from his people that when conflict arose he had few friends to come to his aid.

Pastors like that remind me of the pompous and obstinate preacher that the church couldn't get rid of. Finally one day he received and accepted a call from another church. The day he resigned he said, "Jesus led me here when I became your pastor three years ago, and now Jesus is leading me away." The chairman of the deacons allegedly announced, "Let's all stand and sing, 'What a Friend We Have in Jesus.'"

Listen! You can't act like a skunk without someone getting wind of it. After a while people know what you are, for good or for bad. If you are their friend things will go much better for you.

Six, listen to and learn from your critics. I have often told my staff that our critics are our friends if we respond to them in the right way. They keep us on our toes. They keep us honest. They make us examine our position on every issue to make sure we are right.

Perhaps the most dangerous thing that could happen to me as a leader would be for people never to question me or challenge me on any proposal. Without that prospect I would make more mistakes than I already do.

General Dwight D. Eisenhower reportedly would not make a tactical decision until he found someone who strongly opposed it. He wanted to see any weakness before proceeding. This policy works in churches, too.

The best deacon body or church board is not one where everyone plays follow-the-leader. A church that always votes unanimously the pastor's way will only be as strong as the pastor's personality. When the pastor is overwhelmed, run-down, and needs guidance, a collection of clones won't be adequate. So, respect your critics.

Of course, you cannot be all things to all people all the time. The problem is deciding which criticisms are valid and which are unjustified. It requires a tough hide and a sensitive heart. A few specific guidelines won't hurt. Here are three things you need to consider in distinguishing fair from unfair attacks—you need to consider the source, the number, and the circumstances.

First, consider the source.—Who is saying it? Are they well intended? Are they committed to ministry? Do they want what is best for the church? Or, are they just complainers?

Lyndon Johnson used to tell of a farm dog on the front porch baying plaintively.

"What's the matter with that hound?" asked a visitor.

"Laying on a cocklebur," said the laconic farmer.
"Why don't he git up?"
"Cause he druther howl."
There are people like that in almost every church.

Second, consider the number.—Solitary shots should be ignored, but when they come from several directions, it is time to pay attention. As someone once said, "If one calls thee a donkey, ignore him. If two call thee a donkey, look for hoofprints. If three call thee a donkey, get thee a saddle."

Third, consider the circumstances.—Criticism may tell you more about the person voicing it than about yourself or the issue. It may be an indication of a deeper problem. Is the criticism fair or is it a sign something more is involved? Sometimes the person is having health problems or domestic problems or financial problems or they are frustrated in some other way and they are taking it out on you. Sometimes the person has a hidden agenda and the real issue has not surfaced. So, when you face a critic, try to look behind the scenes, try to discern what is going on in that person's life, and see if the problem is really the problem or if the problem is disguising the problem.

Whatever the source or number of circumstances, a standard reply to every criticism probably ought to be, "You may be right." You haven't conceded a thing. But it does give you time to mull over what the critic has said and it tells the critic that you are taking the observation seriously.

Winning Friends, Influencing People

Finally, confront people when necessary. There are times when in spite of everything you do, confrontation is unavoidable and it is the only way to resolve an issue. John decided that was the approach needed with Diotrephes. So he said, "If I come I will remember his deeds" (v. 10). John planned to confront Diotrephes face to face, and settle the matter. Confrontation is one way you deal with conflict in the church and sometimes the only way.

None of us like unpleasant confrontations but there are times

WORKING WITH THE POWER STRUCTURE OF THE CHURCH 57

when there is no other choice. By refusing to face up to a troublesome issue in the church, you may only be allowing the problem to become worse.

Confrontation is caring enough about another person to place the conflict on the table and talk about it. When you have conflict that leads to confrontation the most important thing is to make sure that you handle the confrontation properly. When criticized by people, our normal response is to become upset or defensive. And when we feel threatened we usually wind up dousing the fire with gasoline. The confrontation with critics has to be carried out in love—smart love.

In a situation where one person feels another has offended him, Jesus taught that the aggrieved individual should first go and discuss the problem with the other person. If the person listens to you, you have won your brother over.

If he does not listen, the offended one should take one or two fellow believers who can help arbitrate the dispute and speak to the one at fault. If he does not listen to them, then the one who feels sinned against should tell it to the assembly of believers. Only then, if he refuses to listen, is the church to withdraw fellowship (Matt. 18:15-17). Jesus' teaching can be broken down into five suggestions about how to confront people properly.

1. *Go privately.*—Jesus said when you have a difference with a person go and tell it "between thee and him alone" (v. 15). Go to the person privately, one to one, lay the problem before him and see if you can resolve it. It needs to be a setting where no one is likely to lose face—a private, unhurried conversation is most effective in restoring relationships.

2. *Go promptly.*—Long-standing disagreements and unresolved situations can fester and grow. Jesus said in the Sermon on the Mount, "Agree with thine adversary quickly" (Matt. 5:25). The apostle Paul said, "Let not the sun go down upon your wrath" (Eph. 4:26). They both say we should deal with our differences quickly.

3. *Go peacefully.*—Jesus said if the confrontation is successful, "thou hast gained thy brother." That is always the goal. The

object is not to win the argument. It is to win a friend. It is to change an adversary into an ally.

4. *Go prayerfully.*—That means you go in the spirit of the Lord Jesus. Dallas businessman, Fred Smith, said in the context of conflict, "If I cannot win in the spirit of Christ, I should lose. It is God's will for me to lose." It is never God's will for us to have an un-Christlike spirit. If we cannot win a confrontation in the spirit of Christ, then we ought not to win.

5. *Go persistently.*—You don't go just once and say, "Well, I've done my duty. They won't be reconciled and I'll handle it my way from here on out." No, you should go first by yourself and if that doesn't work, ask "one or two more" to go with you to help arbitrate. If you still cannot resolve the issue then the church should become the supreme court and settle the matter.

Differences are inevitable within a local church. But it is not our differences that bring shame upon our Lord, and the larger community of believers, it is the way we handle them.

The good news is that by the grace of God, we can learn to love one another and live together in peace. One of the greatest evidences of this is what happened in the life of the man who wrote the Epistle of 3 John. What do we call the apostle John? John is known as "the apostle of love." But early in his life Jesus referred to him and his brother James as "The Sons of Thunder." You can guess why, can't you? It was because they had stormy dispositions. They would cloud up and rain all over you in a minute. But by the grace of God, "the thunderstorm boys" were turned into men of love and graciousness when Jesus became real to them. Thus the hot-headed fisherman became the warmhearted apostle. And what the Lord Jesus did in the life of John the apostle, He can do in your life and in your church. And when He does, it will be a better day for the kingdom of God.

5
When Workers Can't Work Together

William Lloyd Phelps of a bygone era once stated, "The greatest art is the art of living together." Perhaps that art is more tested in staff relations than any other area in the church.

Working together in harmony has long been a problem. As far back as Paul and Barnabas, the first missionary team, people in God's work have had to deal with it. The Bible records an account of this first staff conflict in Acts 15:36-41.

Following the Jerusalem conference and an extended stay in Antioch, Paul suggested to Barnabas that they revisit the churches they had established and the people they had won to Christ on their first missionary journey to see how they were doing. Barnabas apparently shared Paul's concern for the young converts and wanted to take John Mark with them. But, Paul recalling that Mark, who had accompanied them on their first journey, returned home after their second or third stop, did not think it was a good idea and strongly objected. Mark's reason for deserting was not given. Perhaps he was simply homesick. Perhaps it was fear of persecution. Perhaps it was an inner conviction that he was not called to foreign mission service. Whatever the reason, Paul took the defection very hard and did not like the idea of taking a quitter with them.

The upshot of this disagreement was that the contention between them was so sharp "they departed asunder one from the other" (v. 39). They could no longer work together as a missionary team. So Barnabas took Mark and sailed to Cyprus and Paul chose Silas and returned to the churches as they had planned.

These words record for us a contention between two of the best men and most intimate apostles of Jesus Christ. We must not smooth down this conflict to indicate that it was a small disagreement or a minor difference of opinion. The Scriptures say the contention was "sharp." That means it was keen, cutting, and heated. The tempers of both men were ruffled. The altercation between them was so fierce and fiery that the tie of old friendship gave way, and they could no longer work together. The words "departed asunder" are a translation of one Greek word that means "to rend, to tear, to rip." The tension was so severe that the missionary team split.

That this experience should happen at all, and especially between these two men at that crucial time in church history, is one of the most surprising and improbable matters in the New Testament. There are several reasons why this is so.

To begin with, they were both good men. They loved Christ, they loved souls, and they loved each other. We are first introduced to Barnabas when, early in the life of the church, he sold his possessions and gave all he had to meet the needs of others. His real name was Joseph, but the disciples nicknamed him Barnabas, "the son of encouragement." This suggests that he was a kind, sympathetic, and optimistic person. He was always reaching out to others to help them. When the church at Antioch began to grow it was Barnabas whom the apostles sent to supervise that work. There it was spoken of him, "He was a good man, and full of the Holy Ghost and of faith: and much people were added unto the Lord" (Acts 11:24).

And Paul, more than any other person, was responsible for honeycombing the Roman Empire with the gospel. Again and again, he laid his life on the line for the cause of Christ. There is no doubt about it, these were two good men.

Moreover, they were old friends. Some scholars believe that Paul and Barnabas had been schoolmates together at the feet of Gamaliel. It was Barnabas who gave Paul his start in Christian service. When Paul returned to Jerusalem from Damascus, it was Barnabas who took him by the hand and introduced him to the skeptical apostles who otherwise would have recoiled from him in horror.

When the work at Antioch grew to the point that an assistant was needed, Barnabas traveled to Tarsus and enlisted Paul. They were companions on the first long and perilous missionary journey. And together they had been chosen by the church at Antioch to represent them at the Jerusalem council that settled the great ecclesiastical dispute concerning salvation.

And finally, the contention was over such a seemingly small matter, especially when you consider what they had been through together. At Antioch they had worked as a pastoral team to build a great missionary church. On their first missionary journey they had withstood bigoted Jews, idolatrous Gentiles, and angry mobs. At the Jerusalem council they had stood side by side against the Judaizers. They had gone through all of that with unbroken unanimity of soul, and now the mere question of whether or not John Mark should accompany them on their proposed journey broke the harmony of their fellowship.

That is how it so often is. The small concerns of life have generally a greater power to try the temper than the great matters. Call people together to discuss small stuff, and they will quarrel; call them to work on a tremendous project, and they will be cordial and unanimous. The little things annoy.

"How," you ask, "could this kind of thing happen?" It is because the best of people are not infallible. A good person does not mean a faultless one. The best of persons can be stubborn, strong-minded, opinionated, and unbending at times, and sometimes they merely have honest differences. They don't always share the same goals or the same philosophy of ministry. Paul seemed to be committed to evangelism and to church planting, while Barnabas was more people oriented. To Paul it seemed the *work* was most important; to Barnabas the *workers* were most important. Moreover, in this instance they seemingly took it on themselves to decide the matter of whether or not Mark should accompany them.

When it came time for the church at Antioch to send out

missionaries the Holy Spirit said, "Separate me Barnabas and Saul for the work whereunto I have called them" (Acts 13:2). When the Jerusalem council issued its verdict they said, "It seemed good to the Holy Spirit and to us" (15:28, NIV). But, in this decision between Paul and Barnabas concerning John Mark there seems to have been no special direction at all. It was left to their own judgment and wisdom. Many such questions in the Christian life seemingly are left entirely to our discretion. The Lord does not exclude human judgment and personalities in His work.

Obviously, for whatever the reason, one or both of these men were resolved, come what may, to have his own way. They would rather have their own way than to have the companionship of each other and so came alienation and separation.

Who was at fault? We are bound to ask that. We cannot be sure. Apparently the church at Antioch took Paul's side for they commended him to the grace of God. But, Mark's later development proves that Barnabas was also right. It is possible then that they were both right. Maybe Mark needed the sternness of Paul and the kindness of Barnabas. It could be that the hardness of Paul brought out the moral courage and greater diligence in him. And the tenderness of Barnabas gave Mark back his self-respect. We do know the outcome was good, for Mark later became a faithful servant of God.

If this experience had ended here, it would have been sad indeed. But, apparently and happily, they had not departed long before every particle of animosity went out and we find Paul referring kindly to both Mark and Barnabas. One reference to the church in Corinth suggests that Barnabas continued to do the work of an evangelist and still practice the principle to which he and Paul adhered when they were together, supporting himself by manual labor (1 Cor. 9:6). The tone of the reference implies that there were relations of mutual respect. We can at least believe that the two men still thought highly of each other and honored each other for their work's sake even though they found it better to labor apart. Did Paul ever change his attitudes toward Mark? Yes! In two of his letters Paul sends greetings to Mark which leads us to believe he was associated with Paul in the work at Ephesus (Philem. 24; Col. 4:10). And in 2 Timothy Paul asks Timothy to bring Mark with him when he comes for Mark is now useful to Paul in the ministry (4:11).

What happened to Paul and Barnabas can happen to us. People who have worked together in God's service, even on a church staff, can have such conflicts and disagreements that they can no longer continue to work together.

Sometimes it is because they have honest differences. Sometimes it is because they are stubborn and unbending. Sometimes it is because they have different philosophies and goals. But, for whatever reason, it can and does happen.

If this experience had to happen, I am glad the Holy Spirit saw fit to have it recorded. For it reminds me that conflicts can occur in such a way that it doesn't destroy either the workers or the work of God. The workers can split without the church splitting. The question is not, "Do disagreements come?" But, rather, "How do we handle them?" "How do we manage them today so as to not hurt one another or the work of God?" It is imperative that we know this. If the pastor does not maintain good staff relations, then division can occur in the congregation and it will find itself dissipating its best energy on infighting. To this end I offer seven suggestions.

Play Hard or Play Elsewhere

First, begin with a clear understanding. Good staff relations like good marriages begin with a clear understanding from the beginning. This makes a good job description essential. But, beyond this, you should talk candidly about your philosophy of ministry, your goals, and your expectations. You want as few surprises as possible after the honeymoon is over.

If you expect people to be at work at a specific time, tell them so. If you expect them to make prospect visits each week, tell them so. If you expect them to plan and live within their budget, tell them so. If you want only a certain kind of music, tell them so.

As they say, "Don't assume nothing!" Don't assume that a staff person comes to work on time, prays, tithes, visits, wins others to Christ, or that their wives attend Sunday night and Wednesday night services. Talk about those things in advance and you will save yourself and others a lot of grief.

There is a temptation for us to oversell ourselves and our church when we are talking to prospective staff. Some pastors in their eagerness to induce a staff person to join them, and some staff persons in their eagerness to move, do not tell the truth. It is better to say to the person, "This is the direction we are going. If you are going in the same direction, we would love to have you hop on," rather than to take on people who will not be happy. They need to know the ground rules before they join up.

There are a lot of things I like about Jimmy Johnson, the coach of the Dallas Cowboys. One is his straightforwardness with his players. At the outset of his first three-week practice, Johnson's message to the Cowboys was simple and straightforward. "Play hard or play elsewhere."

If that's how you feel about your staff team, tell them up front. Staff people are easier to get than they are to get rid of. What J. Lynn Elder said of choosing pastors can be said of choosing other staff: "Many choose their pastor in haste and repent at leisure."

Of course, sometimes you inherit a staff. What do you do then? Do you remember the old advice from Machiavelli? "The first duty of the new king is to destroy the family of the old prince." That's the way some pastors feel about existing staff, especially those pastors who want to be "king." They come to a new field and want to "surplus" everyone connected with the old regime.

I don't concur with that philosophy in the church. You should first make every effort to work together. But, if in time the staff person does not share your philosophy of ministry, if they will not pursue the goals of the church, or if they will not work under your leadership, then they need to leave. Even then, be kind, gentle, and patient. Give the person time to get relocated. It takes time to find another place and we owe each other that time.

Communications and Staff Relations

Second, keep up good communications. Dr. Othal Feather, longtime professor of Christian Education at Southwestern Baptist Theological Seminary, told me that he once had a student who, upon completion of his seminary work, went to serve on the staff of a church in my hometown of Port Arthur. After a while Dr. Feather received a call from the pastor reporting things were not working out. He couldn't get along with the young man and wanted Dr. Feather to help the man move.

A little later word also came from the former student asking Dr. Feather to help him find a new place to serve. Dr. Feather was scheduled to be in that area for a conference and while there learned that these men were not having regular staff meetings. So there was very little communication. Before the conference was over the pastor asked, "Dr. Feather, what's wrong with us?" Dr. Feather responded, "You two don't know each other. You need to have a weekly staff meeting. You need to talk together, visit together, and pray together." They began and a few months later Dr. Feather received a second letter from the pastor saying, "Don't recommend _____, he's the greatest."

When I was pastor at Green Acres we had two staff retreats each year. One was for dreaming; the other was for calendar planning. Our entire church program was planned and calendared for the year. Once it had been approved I expected it to be carried out. We then had weekly staff meetings to review, update, and discuss what we were doing.

Beyond that, I had an open-door policy to all the staff at all times. And it was not an open door to a closed mind. I listened and was ready to help in any way I could.

The late Bill Veeck, owner of three different baseball teams, was one of the most innovative men ever to be associated with the game. He really cared about his players and their families, as well as the fans. When he bought the Cleveland Indians in 1946 the first action he made was to take off the door to his office so that anybody could walk in.

Now there's a real open-door policy! You may not go that far, but continual communication is essential to good staff relations.

Butter Them Up

Third, build a team spirit, develop a feeling of trust, loyalty, and closeness with your staff. Most often the best way is to build an atmosphere of love and cooperation by praising the staff's strength publicly and by encouraging them privately. So, help each staff person become the best he can be. The finest thing that could happen to the quarterback of a football team is to have an all-pro in every position in front of him. And the finest thing that could happen to a pastor is to have an all-pro quality staff member at every position on his staff. So, dedicate yourself to encouraging, inspiring, training, and motivating your staff to be and do their best. It will pay rich dividends.

You would do well to remember: A man does not live by bread alone. He needs buttering up once in a while.

Bent Out of Shape

Fourth, stay flexible. I read a beatitude recently that I like. It said, "Blessed are the flexible for they shall not be bent out of shape." If you are always getting bent out of shape by people, maybe it's because you are too rigid.

It helps when we recognize and accept the fact that we do not all have the same gifts, abilities, or talents. We can thank God for our diversities as well as our similarities and within reason, we should allow a person to be themselves and give them the freedom to develop as God wants them to be. Things don't always have to be done exactly our way to be done acceptably. And we can be flexible on some decisions. When challenged on an issue some pastors react by retaliating or at least refusing on principle to compromise. They feel they have to come across forcefully to maintain their position of authority or else they'll be disregarded. But the opposite happens. They diminish their authority by pushing too hard. Real authority comes from proven credibility and caring.

Unless they are mindless, spineless, your staff will disagree with you. As someone has said, "The person who agrees with everything you say . . . either isn't paying attention or else plans to sell you something."

Remember that love "suffereth long and is kind." Being patient, not getting upset, being philosophical, being charitable will go a long way toward making you loved and respected by your staff and your people.

Pray Together and Stay Together

Fifth, pray together. In our churches we often pray for the sick, for the lost, for the bereaved. But too often, as a staff, we do not pray for one another.

Years ago I heard the supposedly true story of a pastor who had a woman in his church who didn't like anything he did. She didn't like his sermons. She didn't like the way he dressed. She didn't like the way his children behaved. And she didn't like the program he proposed. She had a cantankerous spirit and was a thorn in his side from the minute he arrived.

He tried to talk with her on several occasions but she would not communicate. He did everything he knew how to do but there seemed to be no way to get along with her.

One day he was visiting in her neighborhood and decided to go by her house. Her car was parked in the driveway so he determined to visit her and see if they could work out their problems.

He rang the doorbell but no one answered. He then knocked on the door, thinking the doorbell might be out of order. But still she did not answer. When you've knocked on as many doors as most preachers you can almost always tell when somebody is inside. It is like a sixth sense. And he was sure she was at home.

So, he went around to the backdoor and knocked again. He called the lady by name saying, "It's the pastor and I would like to talk to you for a minute." But still there was no response.

He went back to the front door again and decided to ring the doorbell one more time. Still there was no answer. Then on an impulse, he said, "I dropped down on my knees and looked through the keyhole." And, what do you suppose he saw? He said, "I saw an eye staring right back at me."

He continued, "She then opened the door and we were both embarrassed." Then he said, "I looked at her and said, 'Isn't it interesting that the first time we got down on our knees together we saw eye to eye?'"

There is more truth than fiction to that. If we would pray more together we would more likely stay together longer. By the way, I heard about another preacher who, while visiting some of his "flock," knocked on the door of a church member but got no answer. He was a bit put out because he could hear footsteps and knew the lady of the house must be there. So he went around to her garden door and knocked again. When she did not answer this time he left his card with a note that read: "Behold, I stand at the door and knock: if any man hear my voice, and open the door, I will come into him" (Rev. 3:20). The next Sunday, as the members were leaving the church, the woman who had refused to answer the door handed the preacher a note that read, "I heard thy voice in the garden, and I was afraid, because I was naked; and I hid myself" (Gen. 3:10).

Care Enough to Confront

Sixth, confront candidly and kindly when necessary. None of us like unpleasant confrontations but there are times when there is no other choice. By refusing to face up to a troublesome issue you may only be allowing the problem to become worse.

When you confront, speak candidly. Some time ago I received word that a fellow pastor in our association had been publicly critical of me. Since we had never had any dealings with each other I knew it had to be his problem, so I paid no attention to it. When it happened a second time, I still ignored it. When it happened the third time I called him on the phone and asked him to have lunch with me.

After a pleasant visit, I said to him, "Is there some contention between us?" He denied there was a problem, but the sheepish look on his face betrayed him. I knew he was not being honest.

I then told him what I had heard and said, "Since we are brothers, I thought we ought to talk about it person-to-person." We then discussed the problem and parted as friends.

Several suggestions about confrontation emerge from this experience.

1. Take the initiative.
2. Pick a time when you will be unhurried and a place where no one will be embarrassed.
3. Never accuse, rather ask questions that get to the heart of the matter. This allows you to face the issues without putting the other person on the defensive.
4. Be candid. Be sure you lay all the cards on the table.

A couple of years later this same man resigned his church because of indiscretion with a number of women. As soon as I heard about it I called him for breakfast to express my concern and to offer my help. He said to me, "I knew you would call."

It is possible to confront and still remain friends.

Go Peacefully

Finally, if you cannot agree then you need to part as brothers. Life is too short and the opportunities for service are too numerous for two people to live in misery, tension, and frustration. If you are forced to go, go peacefully. Don't let a conflict embitter you or interfere with your service for God, and don't let it disrupt the fellowship of the church.

Let it be said to the credit of Paul, Barnabas, and Mark that none of them allowed their disagreement to interfere with their service to God. And neither should we. The quarrel led them to abandon their proposed joint journey, but nothing more. All three continued in missions as though nothing had happened. None of them quit. Though they disagreed over one issue, on the most important fact they were agreed, that the missionary endeavors should continue. The net result of this disagreement was a doubling of the personnel in foreign missionary service.

And none of them harbored bitterness or anger. If you do not forgive those who hurt you, and even fire you, you allow them to hurt you twice. Once when they did it, and again and again by your bitterness and anger.

On the plains of western Canada, early in the fall of the year, during the wheat harvest a three-year-old girl wandered from the yard of her farm home, out into the tall grain and became lost. As night fell and the cold became more intense, the child's father and dozens of neighbors searched frantically through the fields in a fruitless effort to find her. Finally one of the men called the search to a halt, and suggested that they all join hands and, like a giant combine, comb through the field. This they did and finally in the bitter-cold hours just before dawn the child's lifeless body was found. The little girl had succumbed to exhaustion and cold. In anguish, the poor grief-stricken father cried out, "Oh, God, if we had only joined hands sooner!" That's what we must do.

I trust that can be true with us also. The whole experience teaches us that no one needs to stay the way one is. A man like John Mark can come back from failure and rejection to usefulness. And a man like Paul can admit his mistake. Our gospel is not only the gospel of redemption for lost souls, but the gospel of redemption for failures and for broken relationships.

6
Spill-over Conflict

John Fawcett was a Baptist preacher in Yorkshire, England, in the latter part of the eighteenth century and the first part of the nineteenth. His salary was equivalent to $200 a year. He received a call, at a much larger salary, from a church in London. He felt justified in accepting the call and resigned his Yorkshire pastorate. His household goods were packed on the wagon; his family was aboard; and the good pastor looked out upon the weeping group of people who had come to tell him good-bye. He had shared his life with them; they had shared their lives with him. The grief that they felt at his leaving and the grief he felt at the thought of leaving caused him to give the word that the household goods be taken back into the parsonage. So there in the small but great fellowship of people who loved him so dearly he remained for the rest of his life. Out of this experience came the hymn "Blest Be the Tie that Binds."

"Blest be the tie that binds
  Our hearts in Christian love;
The fellowship of kindred minds
  Is like to that above.

Before our Father's throne
  We pour our ardent pray'rs;
Our fears, our hopes, our aims are one
  Our comforts and our cares.

We share our mutual woes,
  Our mutual burdens bear;

And often for each other flows
The sympathizing tear.

When we asunder part,
  It gives us inward pain;
But we shall still be joined in heart,
  And hope to meet again.

There is the spirit that ought to characterize the family of God. But, so often, it is not so. As a young staff wife wrote to me recently about her husband, "Kelly knows that the hardest place to work is a church. There are so many conflicts. It seems as though you can never please everyone."

The fact is, Christians have the bewildering capacity to treat one another brutally. There is nothing that can hurt as much as the bile of the brethren.

Christians having a hard time getting along is not new. It has been a problem since the church's inception. The apostle Paul acknowledged this when he wrote to the church at Philippi, "I beseech Euodias, and beseech Syntyche, that they be of the same mind in the Lord. And I entreat thee also, true yokefellow, help those women which labored with me in the gospel, with Clement also, and with other my fellow laborers, whose names are in the book of life" (Phil. 4:2-3).

Euodias and Syntyche were obviously active and well-known members of the church at Philippi. Their Christian faith was not in question. They had "labored" together with Paul and their "names are in the book of life" (v. 3). But they were at odds with one another. Even Christians get crosswise occasionally.

We have no idea what their disagreement was over and it doesn't matter. What matters is that their personal differences were spilling over into the church and it was on the verge of disrupting the entire fellowship.

There were divisions in the churches of Galatia over doctrine. There was division in the church at Corinth over preachers. Here the division seemed to be over a personal conflict between two individuals. This was of grave concern to Paul and he felt it should be of concern to every member of the church.

SPILL-OVER CONFLICT

The apostle Paul offers two admonitions: First, to Euodias and Syntyche he pleads, "Be of the same mind in the Lord." He does not ask them to be of one opinion, of one taste, of one feeling, of one emotion. He asks them to be of one mind and to let that mind be in Christ.

To be of the same mind in Christ doesn't mean we lose our individuality in the church. We can disagree without being disagreeable. We can be brothers without being identical twins. We do not have to see eye to eye in order to walk arm in arm. We should not be afraid of holding different opinions but of harboring unbrotherly attitudes.

But if members of the church have the same mind in Christ they will find that their other differences can not only be solved but in the solving of them the fellowship of the church will be enriched.

Paul's advice to the rest of the congregation was, "help those women" (v. 3). Obviously Euodias and Syntyche needed assistance in reconciling their differences and he pleaded with the church to provide it.

That is often the case in our churches today. Conflict between two individuals can spread throughout the entire congregation. The first thing you know the fellowship is divided not because of deep doctrinal differences but because of family ties and personal friendships. When that happens personal friendships and the church fellowship both suffer.

What could the church at Philippi do to help resolve the differences between these two women? What can we do when there is the danger of spill-over conflict in our churches today? I suggest three things: we can pray for them; we can counsel with them; we can mediate between them.

Pray for Them

First, when conflict between Christians is spilling over into the church we can pray for them. What is prayer?

Prayer is not a blank check on which God's signature appears, guaranteeing us anything on which we may set our hearts. God does not put Himself at the mercy of the whims of finite men and women.

Prayer is not a rabbit's foot or a charm, warranted to preserve us from misfortune. Prayer is not a parachute project to be reserved for use in some extreme emergency.

Prayer is not a child's letter to Santa Claus. It is not just an appeal devoted to securing "things." And prayer, true prayer, is not an attempt to change God's mind, or to bring him around to our way of thinking. "Prayer," wrote Danish philosopher Soren Kierkegaard, "does not change God, but changes him who prays."

Prayer is not an Aladdin's lamp, which by rubbing brings us whatever we may want.

Prayer is not primarily saying or repeating words, even though it may be, "Now I lay me down to sleep," the Lord's Prayer, or the great collects of the prayer book.

Prayer is not trying to bend God's will to our will. "Prayer is not overcoming God's reluctance," said Bishop Trench, "it is laying hold of God's highest willingness."

Prayer is not using God; it is more often to get us in a position where God can use us. Billy Graham tells of watching the deckhands on a great liner as they docked the ship in New York harbor. First, they threw out a rope to the men on the dock. Then, inside the boat the great motors went to work and pulled on the great cable. But of course the pier wasn't pulled out to the ship; the ship was moved snugly up to the pier. Prayer is the rope that pulls God and man together. But it doesn't pull God down to us; it pulls us up to Him.

Prayer is talking with God. Sometimes it is calling on God for help, sometimes it is thanking Him for His blessings, sometimes it is sharing with Him your needs and those of others.

Sharing with God the needs of others is called intercession. This is one of the greatest kinds of prayer, for in it you are thinking and affecting the lives of others. Some anonymous poet wrote of the power of intercession:

SPILL-OVER CONFLICT

> There's no weapon half so mighty
> As the intercessors bear;
> Nor a broader field of service
> Than the ministry of prayer.

This kind of prayer we should offer for our fellow Christians who are estranged.

Does prayer really work? Millions of voices through the ages have said so. "If you make a habit of sincere prayer," wrote the distinguished physician Alexis Carrel, "your life will be very noticeable and profoundly altered. Prayer is the most powerful form of energy that one can generate."

I could not put it any better than the early church father, Chrysostom, who said, "The potency of prayer had subdued the strength of fire; it had bridled the rage of lions, hushed anarchy to rest, extinguished wars, appeased the elements, expelled demons, burst the chains of death, expanded the gates of heaven, assuaged diseases, repelled frauds, rescued cities from destruction, stayed the sun in its course, and arrested the progress of the thunderbolt. Prayer is an all-sufficient panoply, a treasure undiminished, a mine which is never exhausted, a sky unobscured by clouds, a heaven unfurled by storm. It is the roof, the fountain, the mother of a thousand blessings."

From the first pages of Genesis to the last words of Revelation we see scriptural evidence that God answers prayer. Bishop J. C. Ryle adds these insights: "Prayer has obtained things that seemed impossible and out of reach. It has won victories over fire, air, earth and water. Prayer opened the Red Sea. Prayer brought water from the rock and bread from heaven. Prayer made the sun stand still. Prayer brought fire from the sky on Elijah's sacrifice. Prayer overthrew the army of Sennacherib. Prayer has healed the sick. Prayer has raised the dead. Prayer has produced the conversion of countless souls."

Indeed, God has said nothing lies beyond the potential of prayer. So, let us pray. Especially let us pray for one another. You can do more to effect reconciliation between people after you pray, but you cannot do more before you pray. It can be a powerful factor in reconciling estranged Christians.

Counsel with Them

Second, when conflict between two Christians is spilling over into the church we can counsel with them. We all need the counsel of others.

Solomon, one of the wisest men who ever lived, wrote, "Where no counsel is, the people fall: but in the multitude of counselors there is safety" (Prov. 11:14). And again, "For by wise counsel thou shalt make thy war: and in multitude of counselors there is safety" (24:6).

Solomon's own son failed to heed the advice of his father and lost his leadership in Israel because of it. When Rehoboam was appointed king he received wise counsel from the elders of Israel. But, he promptly ignored it and did the very opposite. The end result was that Israel revolted against him and made Jeroboam their king.

We cannot guarantee that people will listen to us when we go to them, but we have the obligation to go anyway. We dare not allow church division to go on unchecked. We are honor bound to do what we can to confront it and to correct it.

What can we say to our fellow Christians who are estranged from one another? For one thing we can encourage them to pray for one another. Artist Whitman tells how prayer for others helps. In fact, he said prayer is most powerful when it is prayed for one's enemies. He said, "Once I couldn't get an injury done me out of my mind. Leafing casually through a book in the library, I came across an arresting phrase, 'If you will understand your enemy, you can love him.' Praying for light, I saw how miserable my enemy's childhood had been, and I saw that, in our relationship, I was to blame too, even if unintentionally. I prayed that life would be kinder to her than it had been for so long. Praying so, I scarcely noticed when the corroding injury went out of my heart." That can happen to anyone.

We can remind them of the importance of love. Love is at the heart of our faith. Jesus said it was the distinguishing mark of His followers. If we Christians cannot live together in love, how can we convince the world we serve a God of love? And, as you know, love reduces friction to a fraction.

SPILL-OVER CONFLICT

We can ask them, "How can we honestly say to political systems, 'You must learn to live together'; how can we say to management and labor, 'You must learn to work together'; how can we expect race and race to have fellowship in the world at large if individuals from these groups cannot find peace and harmony within the churches? How can we plead with the world to be reconciled unless we plead with one another to be reconciled?"

There are mutual interests that should draw each of these groups together on the level of politics, business, culture, education, and so on. But surely there is no motive in any of these areas that can match the motive that churches have for knowing the spirit of reconciliation. Our motivation finds its source at the cross and in the One who suffered there that we all might be one.

There will be differences of opinion among the followers of Christ within the fellowship of the church; of course there will be. It was true in the early churches; it is true in the later churches. This is not only to be expected, it is to be encouraged. This can bring new light, new truth; the fellowship can be enriched by it. Within the fellowship of the church is the one place that it should be possible for persons to disagree without being disagreeable, to differ and be creative in the difference. But we must not allow differences to be disruptive to the fellowship. We must counsel when possible and confront when necessary to keep personal conflict from spilling over into the church.

Mediate Between Them

Finally, when conflict between two Christians is spilling over into the church we can mediate between them. Our generation is familiar with the role of mediators. As I write this, the Dallas/Fort Worth International Airport hired a mediator to help resolve airport expansion problems with the city of Irving.

A mediator is one who interposes between parties at variance to reconcile them. In disputes between labor and management the court often appoints a mediator to assist in resolving them. In conflicts between nations, the General Council of the United

Nations sometimes serves as a mediator. Mediators are vital to a peaceful and orderly society.

Mediation plays an important part in the Christian life. The apostle Paul wrote, "For there is one God, and one mediator between God and men, the man Jesus Christ" (1 Tim. 2:5). Through His life, death, and resurrection Jesus bridged the chasm of sin that separates man from God and made possible our reconciliation to Him. The heart of the gospel is, "God was in Christ, reconciling the world unto himself" (2 Cor. 5:19).

We who have been reconciled to God are not only to help the lost to be reconciled to God, but we are also to help mediate between our brothers who are estranged from one another. In telling us how to settle disputes among ourselves Jesus gave four clear steps.

- First, if another wrongs you, you should go to that person and discuss the matter between the two of you alone.
- Second, if that does not succeed in resolving the difference, you should then take one or two others to serve as mediators and witnesses.
- Third, if reconciliation is still not achieved because of his/her unwillingness, the matter should then be presented to the church for final arbitration.
- Fourth, the unreasonable and unbending and unrepentant brother should be treated as an unbeliever.

I cannot overstate the importance of our being reconciled to one another. Paul said we are not to let the sun go down on our wrath. And he adds that we are to give no opportunity to the devil. When we refuse to seek reconciliation, we are opening the door for the devil, our fiercest enemy.

History records that on the day before Trafalgar, the great sea battle, Nelson called a conference of the senior officers of his ship, *Victory*. He noticed the absence of Captain Rotherham, the commander of the flagship of Admiral Collinwood. He inquired the reason for Rotherham's absence and was told by Collinwood that

SPILL-OVER CONFLICT

he and Rotherham were not on good terms with each other. "Terms!" shouted Nelson, "not on good terms with each other!" The conference was adjourned and a messenger sent for Rotherham. When he came, Nelson took Rotherham and Collinwood and pointed out to them the long line of French and Spanish ships on the horizon, under the skilled command of Villeneuve. "Look!" he demanded. "Yonder is your enemy. Shake hands like Englishmen." They did so and in the face of a fierce enemy became friends again.

That's what we must do as brothers in Christ—recognize who the real enemy is and be both reconciled and reconcilers.

On a golfing outing in Hawaii, Dr. Darold H. Morgan, my predecessor at the Annuity Board, was placed with a threesome from Japan. As he introduced himself to his Japanese partners, one of them asked, "Are you a Christian?"

When Morgan answered he was, one of the Japanese men said, "I am a Buddhist, but I like Christians. You are so kind to one another."

The man had obviously seen true Christianity in action. I wish everyone could see that and say that about Christians. And they could if we would eliminate spill-over conflict in the church.

7
When Others Hurt Us

All my life I have heard that two things are certain—death and taxes. Another thing needs to be added to that list of sure things—hurts. It is inevitable as we go through life that people will hurt us.

Sometimes they hurt us accidently; sometimes it is intentional. Sometimes they hurt us by what they do; sometimes it is by what they say. Sometimes the wounds are superficial and heal quickly; at other times they are deep and the scars remain a lifetime. But mark it down somewhere. People do hurt us.

What do we do when others hurt us? How should we react? We need to know. The apostle Paul gives us a hint when he writes, "Alexander the coppersmith did me much evil. The Lord reward him according to his works: Of whom be thou ware also; for he hath greatly withstood our words" (2 Tim. 4:14-15).

These verses are a part of the biographical writings of the apostle Paul. They are like a page out of his spiritual diary. As he recounts to Timothy some of his experiences as a missionary he mentions that a man named Alexander, who was a coppersmith by trade, had hurt him deeply.

What did Alexander do to the apostle Paul? We have no idea. And Paul does not tell us. The Greek word translated "evil" can mean depraved or injurious or wicked. The Greek word translated "much" can mean a large amount, or often or many times. Obviously what Alexander did to Paul was no small, incidental thing. It was deeply hurtful and perhaps done repeatedly.

Whatever it was he did Paul does not amplify it or dwell on it.

If I had been the one hurt and telling the story, I would have gone into the greatest of detail. I would have wanted everyone to know every detail of what Alexander did and how deeply I was hurt by it. But not the apostle Paul. He never felt sorry for himself. He never attempted to gain sympathy for himself. He harbored no anger or bitterness over what happened to him.

Paul had obviously developed the ability to remember the best and forget the rest in life. He simply related this incident to warn Timothy to watch out for Alexander. And, in so doing, gives us an example of how to respond to the hurts of life.

What happened to Paul can happen to us. People can and often do hurt us deeply and repeatedly. They exclude us from their group. They fire us from a job. They block us from a promotion. They criticize us unjustly. They say things that are harsh and cruel.

The person who wrote, "Sticks and stones may hurt my bones but words can never hurt me," has not had said about him what I've had said about me. Words, spoken harshly and critically, can wound deeply.

When things like that happen we need to know how to respond. We need to know. What do we do when people hurt us? This experience from the life of the apostle Paul helps us to know what to do and how to respond.

First, when others hurt us, we should not be surprised. Hurts are a normal part of life. We should expect them.

Second, we should not allow hurts to fester into bitterness and resentment. We must learn to remember the best and forget the rest.

Finally, we shouldn't try to get even with the person who has hurt us. We should leave vengeance to God.

It's a Fact of Life

What do we do when people hurt us? First, don't be surprised. Paul mentions his experience with Alexander in such a matter of fact way that we know he knew it was a normal part of life. He accepted hurts as a part of the price of living and serving God.

Many people are hypersensitive to jealousy and criticism. They are extremely touchy when adverse judgment is leveled at them. They take appreciation for granted and they regard criticism as impertinence.

However, the normal person comes much nearer to taking criticism for granted and regarding appreciation as velvet. In fact, if we are healthy minded, we will understand that such hurts are a part of life and if we have a well-integrated personality we will accept them without surprise.

From this week's newspaper—and almost any week's newspaper—there are illustrations of how none of us are immune to hurtful deeds and words. The first is about Greg Norman who, despite playing only seventeen tournaments, led the PGA tour money list for the second time in 1990 with earnings of $1,165,477.

In his thirties, Norman, with blond hair, white teeth, and a million-dollar smile, is perhaps the world's most marketable athlete.

He has a helicopter, a 52-foot fishing boat, a Palm Beach mansion, multiple Ferraris, an income of $8-10 million, commercials, endorsements, looks, and critics.

Almost everyone agrees that Norman has a great personality, he's fun to be with, but there's plenty of resentment festering over the overwhelming publicity and the lucrative endorsements he receives compared to the number of tournaments (nine) he's won.

Just one evidence is despite the fact that he won the Vardon trophy for lowest scoring average (69.10) for the second consecutive year in 1990 it wasn't sufficient to satisfy his peers, who voted Wayne Levi the PGA Tour Player of the Year.

To his fans Norman is affectionately referred to as "The Great White Shark." But one anonymous player called him "The Great White Carp," and another dubbed him "The Great White Charlatan."

Norman has no reply for his critics. He says, "Everybody is entitled to their opinion. You've got to be a little thick skinned and accept the fact that some people might not like you, like the way you are and like what you've done.

"As a great example," he said, "I was playing with (actor) Jack Lemmon recently and we were talking about this and he said he has critics. I said, 'How in the world can you have critics?' And he said I wouldn't believe the number of his critics. It's a fact of life."

The same week, when President Bush was hospitalized with what at first was feared to be a heart attack, critics immediately began a verbal attack on Vice-President Quayle. Despite the fact that President Bush said, "He is doing a first-class job," critics severely questioned Quayle's ability to lead the nation if the President should be incapacitated. Even his children, he said, were forced to defend him to their classmates.

Quayle's response? "The press barbs and TV jokes hurt. No one likes ridicule—especially the proud person that I am. But it goes with the territory. So I will plow ahead and ignore it. Since it's free and unsolicited," he said, "I have the privilege of ignoring it."

I like that. I really do. We always have the choice of making the same kind of response to those who hurt us. After a man had verbally attacked an old sage he responded, "Son, if someone declined to accept a present, to whom would it belong?" The man answered, "To him who offered it."

"And so," said the old man, "I decline to accept your abuse."

The world is full of people who established their worth by degrading others. They have pockets and purses full of put-downs—and they'll hand them to anyone.

Refuse to accept their insults, even when hurled under the guise of love. By ignoring them, you'll reduce tension, strengthen your relationships, and increase your joy.

But remember Jack Lemmon's words. They will help you handle life's hurts. Criticism is a fact of life. It comes to everybody. So when it happens to us we should not be surprised.

Anger Is Like Acid

Second, when others hurt you don't become bitter or resentful. Don't dwell on what they did. Forgive them and forget it. That's what Paul did.

You will notice that Paul does not elaborate on what Alexander did to him. He simply relates the experience as a warning to

Timothy and then quickly moves on to other matters. There is no nursing or rehearsing of the evil deed on Paul's part. There is no hint of bitterness or resentment in his heart.

One of the surest signs that a hurt has turned to bitterness and resentment is that we keep reviewing in our mind and rehashing in our conversation the wrong we have suffered.

There are people who do that, you know. They are like the woman Robert Burns told about in his poem, *Tam o'Shanter*. She stayed busy all through the day, "Nursing her wrath to keep it warm." They nurse their grievances, and seem to derive some sort of fiendish delight from so doing.

But the effects of hate and bitterness are deadly. They are like acid. They do more damage to the vessel in which they are stored than the object upon which they are poured. Physically they increase your blood pressure. Emotionally they contribute to depression. Spiritually they hinder worship and prayer. And socially they make you sour and unpleasant to be around.

Charley Reese warned us well when he said, "It is never wise to wish for another's misfortune. If malice or envy were tangible and had shape, it would be the shape of a boomerang." I saw a television movie that pointed out the devastating effects of hate. It was about a young man who had a love-hate relationship with his father and he was trying desperately to hurt his dad in a business deal. When his stepmother learned of it and chastised him he responded, "I just wanted to beat him once." And she replied, "You haven't beaten him. You have become him."

That may be why former President Richard Nixon, surrounded by his wife, children, and cabinet, walked into the White House press room in August of 1974 to resign under the pressure of Watergate and said to all of us, "Don't ever hate anyone because when you hate them they've got you."

Carrying a grudge is a loser's game. It is the ultimate frustration because it leaves you with more pain than you had in the first place. If you don't forgive those who wrong you, then you allow them to hurt you more than once. They hurt you once when they do what they did to you. And they hurt you again every time you recall it. Your memory becomes a videotape within your soul that plays unending reruns of your pain.

The only way to heal the pain of a past hurt is to forgive the person who hurt you. Why is forgiveness so important? For one thing it heals your memory as you change your perspective. When you release the wrongdoer from the wrong, you cut a malignant tumor out of your inner life. You set a prisoner free—yourself.

And, it's the only way to break the cycle of blame and pain in a relationship. As long as we don't forgive, the cycle goes on and on.

The novel, *Love in the Time of Cholera*, by Laureat Gabriel Garcia Marquez expresses this pattern eloquently. It portrays a marriage that disintegrates over a bar of soap. It was the wife's job to keep the house in order, including the towels, toilet paper, and soap in the bathroom. One day she forgot to replace the soap, and overnight her husband mentioned in an exaggerated way ("I've been bathing for almost a week without any soap"), but that she vigorously denied. Although she had indeed forgotten, her pride was at stake, and she would not back down. For the next seven months they slept in separate rooms and ate in silence.

"Even when they were old and placid," writes Marquez, "they were very careful about bringing it up, for the barely healed wounds could begin to bleed again as if they had been inflicted only yesterday." How can a bar of soap ruin a marriage? Because neither party would say, "Stop. This cannot go on. I'm sorry. Forgive me." Over such trivialities, lifelong relationships crack apart; only forgiveness can halt the widening gap.

Forgiveness breaks the cycle. It does not settle all questions of blame and justice and fairness. To the contrary, often it evades those questions. But it does allow relationships to start over.

So when others hurt you don't allow their wrong to canker into bitterness and resentment. Forgive the one who hurt you so you can heal and be whole again.

An Act of Faith

Third, don't play God. Don't seek to get revenge. Leave that to the Lord.

The apostle Paul says concerning Alexander, "The Lord reward him according to his works." In the original language that statement does not express a wish or a desire. It is simply a statement of fact. Paul is so convinced of the ultimate justice of God that he is not concerned about getting even with Alexander. God will do that. And Paul is willing to trust God's scales of justice.

In the final analysis, forgiveness is an act of faith for all of us. By forgiving another, we are simply trusting that God is a better justice-maker than we are. By forgiving, we leave the fairness for God to work out. We defer to Him the scales of justice. If we try to get even we are playing God.

That's easier said than done. There is a popular saying when someone hurts you: "Don't get mad, get even." That's more my natural inclination.

I can readily identify with Cornelius Vanderbilt, the first American to make a fortune of more than $100 million. To put that century-ago fortune in perspective, the federal budget when he died in 1877 was under $350 million and skilled workers earned $12 a week or $600 a year. Beginning with $100 he borrowed from his mother he built his vast fortune first in the shipping industry and later in railroads. With a drive that would not let him stop he showed a young America what competition was; and dominated the business scene of his day in a way that no person can ever pretend to equal today.

Once, when he was double-crossed by two partners, Vanderbilt went into a towering rage and delivered his most famous and quotable blast: "You have undertaken to cheat me. I won't sue you, for the law is too slow. I'll ruin you."

That's the way I feel when others hurt me. I want to hurt them back.

But the Scriptures are clear. We are to hate evil, be joyful, live in harmony, not be conceited—the list goes on and on. Then appears this verse: "Do not take revenge, my friends, but leave room for

God's wrath, for it is written: 'It is mine to avenge; I will repay,' says the Lord" (Rom. 12:19, NIV).

The sterling exampling of this response in the Bible is Joseph. When he was seventeen years of age he was sold into slavery by his brothers. The slave traders who bought him carried him into Egypt where he became the property of Potiphar, the captain of the pharaoh's guard.

God prospered him and in time he rose to such prominence that he was second in authority only to the pharaoh in Egypt.

When years of famine came to that part of the world, his brothers traveled from Canaan to Egypt to buy grain.

When Joseph recognized them and revealed himself to them they feared him. They were sure he would repay them for their evil. But Joseph convinced them he held no ill will and persuaded them to move their father and their families to Egypt to escape the great famine that would last five more years.

In time, Jacob, their father, died and was taken back to the land of Canaan for burial. With their father gone, the old fears of Joseph's brothers revived. They were sure now that their dad was dead Joseph would get his revenge. Once again, Joseph reassured them with some of the greatest words of the Old Testament, "Fear not: for am I in the place of God? But as for you, you thought evil against me; but God meant it unto good, to bring to pass, as it is this day, to save much people alive. Now therefore fear ye not; I will nourish you, and your little ones. And he comforted them, and spake kindly unto them" (Gen. 50:19-21).

The person who tries to repay evil for evil and wrong for wrong is consciously or unconsciously playing God.

Joseph, like the apostle Paul, had such an absolute confidence in the justice and fairness of God that he was willing to leave the hurts of life in God's hands. That's what we should do.

But Jesus himself is our everlasting example. Peter says of him, "Who, when he was reviled, reviled not again; when he suffered, he threatened not; but committed himself to him that judgeth righteously" (1 Pet. 2:23). That's Christ's way. That should be our way.

So when others hurt you, don't be surprised, don't be bitter, and don't seek revenge.

8
Working Out Doctrinal Differences

Conflict in churches and among Christians often swirls not only around personalities, leadership styles, philosophies of work, and personal biases, but also around doctrinal differences. What we believe we tend to equate with absolute truth, especially in the religious realm. And we often feel compelled to defend our convictions at all costs. These doctrinal differences have resulted not only in the formation of new denominations, but also in bitter strife within congregations and denominations.

If we are going to live together in peace as the family of God we must learn to resolve our major differences and accept the minor ones. But, how do we do that? When two people who are both sincere hold different beliefs on an issue how can they live together in peace? What principles are there to guide us?

We can find them, I think, in the motto of John Amos Comenius, the seventeenth-century Moravian reformer, commonly known as the father of modern education. His motto was: "In essentials, unity; in non-essentials, liberty; in all things, charity."

These three principles can be seen in the proceedings of the first great council of the Christian church, the Jerusalem conference on salvation (Acts 15).

This conference was precipitated by the return of Paul and Barnabas from their first missionary journey where they had met with considerable success among the Gentiles. Then that success brought to a head the most crucial problem in the early church—the relationship between Jewish and Gentile believers and the terms of admission of Gentiles into the Christian fellowship.

WORKING OUT DOCTRINAL DIFFERENCES

The returned missionaries stopped at Antioch, the church that had sent them on their journey, to report on their missionary efforts. During their extended stay in Antioch that conflict over doctrine surfaced. A group of men came from Jerusalem, teaching that—unless the Gentiles committed themselves to the law of Moses by submitting to the ritual of circumcision—they could not be saved. This was contrary to what Paul and Barnabas had taught their converts (i.e., that the door of salvation was through faith alone, Acts 14:27). The teachings of those Judaizers had far-reaching implications. If it were not dealt with swiftly and decisively, it could have split the Christian community into two hostile camps.

Paul and Barnabas immediately recognized the gravity of the matter and vigorously opposed the Judaizers from Jerusalem. The results were they had "no small dissension and disputation" (15:2) with them. The contention soon came to a deadlock, and there seemed to be only one way out. The church would have the issue settled in Jerusalem. So, a delegation was appointed to go there and seek their counsel on the matter. The end result was that Paul and Barnabas traveled to Jerusalem where a solemn assembly of believers was called to resolve the problem.

The church at Jerusalem warmly received the delegation and listened joyfully to the story of their missionary success among the Gentiles. The Judaizers followed them and quickly voiced their opinion: "The Gentiles need to be circumcised and accept the law of Moses just as the Jews" (v. 5, Author).

Then followed an open church meeting where there was "much disputing" (v. 7). It was not a convention of delegates but a meeting of the church. In true democratic fashion, the issue of salvation was openly debated; when the church had heard both sides they voted. The vote was unanimous. They affirmed the truth that God had already revealed (i.e., people are saved by grace through faith without the works of the law). And in kindness but firmness, they resolved the issue for the church once and for all.

Peter was the first to speak. He recalled his own experience in reference to the Cornelius episode, his point being that God had made no distinction between the Jew and the Gentile, but received both by faith, And, in his opinion, they should not "tempt God" by refusing to follow His guidance (vv. 7-11). Paul and Barnabas spoke next, relating their missionary experiences and God's wonderful work of grace among the Gentiles (v. 12).

James, the leader of the church at Jerusalem, and seemingly the presiding officer at the council, spoke last. He summed up what the others had concluded and then appealed to Scripture by quoting the prophet Amos as proof that it had been God's purpose through the ages to call out the Gentiles (Amos 9:1-12). He ended with his opinion that the Jewish Christians should not impose unreasonable and unnecessary demands on Gentile converts (v. 19).

At the same time, the Gentile converts should be requested to respect scruples of the Jewish brethren by avoiding such practices as eating meat that had been offered to idols, or from which the blood had not been drained, and by rejecting the low moral standards of the pagan world. Out of love and respect they should not do those things that were considered an abomination to the Jewish brethren.

James's leadership was apparently not the leadership of power or of official office. It was moral leadership conceded him because he was an outstanding man. He didn't order or dictate—he suggested. He stated in effect, "Wherefore my judgment is . . . I think . . . my opinion is . . . we should not trouble them" (vv. 13-21).

Luke then records, "This pleased the apostles and elders, with the whole church" (v. 22). Once the church had come to its decision it acted with both efficiency and courtesy. It wrote a letter that set out its message and entrusted it to respected leaders—not just Paul and Barnabas, but Judas and Silas, who would translate the cold message of a letter with personal warmth and compassion. A copy of that letter is recorded in verses 24-29.

No conditions would be imposed on Gentile Christians for salvation or for admission to full Christian fellowship, save that provision which God Himself had accepted as sufficient, faith in

Christ. They would not trouble the Gentile converts further, they would not harass them, press them into observances which were not essential to salvation. They would only appeal to their Christian love by asking them to respect the scruples of their Jewish brethren, and their decision was unanimous (v. 25).

Then came a moving, holy moment when they claimed inspiration for this decision by saying, "It seemed good to the Holy Ghost, and to us" (v. 28). The secret of their unanimity was the presence of the Holy Spirit in the assembly. It was not the decision of a man or of a group. It was God's decision.

It is significant that Luke does not record so much the details of their differences as the ultimate harmony of the decision. We must not fail to see that there were many differences, and perhaps in some a touch of bitterness. Yet, at last, there came a wonderful moment when the assembly of Christian believers, with different opinions, after discussion, were able to declare, "It seemed good to the Holy Spirit and to us" (NIV).

The importance of the Jerusalem Conference is seen at three points. *First, it decisively confirmed the principle of salvation by grace. On this they were agreed.* On this they were united. *Second, it affirmed the Christian's freedom from Jewish legalism.* It showed that Christianity by its very nature transcends racial, national, social, and cultural bonds. *Third, it demonstrated a particular method of settling Christian problems, namely by democratic procedure under the guidance of the Holy Spirit.*

Do you see the three principles of Comenius in this experience? They are there, and they are, I believe, the secret for living together with doctrinal differences. They worked in the early church, and they will work for us if we will allow the Holy Spirit to be in control. Look at them and their application more closely.

Things on Which We Can Agree

The first requirement for living in peace when we have doctrinal differences is: "In essentials, unity." The Jerusalem Conference concluded that salvation was by faith alone, apart from works of the law. On this they were agreed. On this they were unanimous.

The Scriptures ask, "Can two walk together except they be agreed?" The answer is an implied "no." So, as we walk and work and worship together there will always be some essentials we must agree on. Clearly, some things are not negotiable. But what are they? While not everyone will agree even on what the essentials are, let me venture four suggestions.

The first nonnegotiable is the lordship of Christ. The theme of the first Christian sermon following the resurrection was "Jesus is Lord" (Acts 2:38). The lordship of Christ was not only the initial confession of the church, it will be the eventual confession of all creation (Phil. 2:9-11), and it is the essential confession of a Christian today (Rom. 10:9-10). On this we must agree.

The inspiration and authority of Scripture are nonnegotiable. The apostle Paul wrote to Timothy, "All scripture is given by inspiration of God, and is profitable for doctrine, for reproof, for correction, for instruction in righteousness" (2 Tim. 3:16).

The word translated "all" means "every single part of the whole." We do not believe parts of Scripture are inspired and other parts aren't. We believe it is all inspired. Since it is all inspired, it is "truth without mixture of error." And since it is truth without mixture of error it is authoritative for our lives. It is the rule and guide for our faith and practice. On that, we must be united.

The way of salvation is not negotiable. The way to be saved is set out in the simplest and clearest way in Paul and Silas' response to the Philippian jailer's question, "Sirs, what must I do to be saved?" Their answer was, "Believe on the Lord Jesus Christ, and thou shalt be saved" (Acts 16:30-31).

Salvation is a gift of God. It comes by grace through faith. It cannot be earned by being good or by being religious (Eph. 2:8-9; Titus 3:5; Gal. 3:11). It cannot be inherited (John 1:13; 3:5); it cannot be purchased (Acts 8:20). It is not a status we achieve. It is what we freely receive when we believe in Jesus Christ. To be saved we must turn from every effort to save ourselves and trust wholly in Jesus Christ who died for our sins, was buried, and was raised again on the third day. That is essential.

The priesthood of the believer is not negotiable. The priesthood of the believer is the belief that every Christian has the right to approach God directly in prayer, in confession of sin, and in understanding and interpreting Scripture for him/herself. It is the belief that no human stands between the believer and God.

In the Old Testament, God ordained the family of Aaron first, and later the tribe of Levi, as His priests. His people were to approach Him through them.

However, when Christ died on the cross the veil of the temple was rent from top to bottom, signifying that the way of direct access into His presence had been opened to all people by God Himself (Luke 23:45).

Jesus Christ has become our High Priest, and through Him we now have access to God without necessity of any human intermediaries (Heb. 4:15-16; 1 Tim. 2:5). Beyond this, He has made each of us a priest unto God (1 Pet. 2:5,9; Rev. 1:6).

For this belief, the right to be our own priest, Felix Manz was drowned in the water of Zurichzee while his mother, standing on the bank, called out to him, "Felix! Don't recant! Don't recant!"

For this right Balthasar Hübmaier was burned at the stake. For this right John Bunyan languished for twelve years in Bedford prison.

For this right Roger Williams was banished from the Massachusetts colony to live in the wilderness among the Indians for two years. For this right 8,000 dissenters died in prison under King Charles II of England. And for this right, for ourselves and others, we must stand today.

On these essentials we must be unified. They are not negotiable.

We've Got to Think

The second requirement for living together in peace with doctrinal differences is "In nonessentials, liberty." The Jerusalem Conference concluded that they would not press the Gentile converts into observances which were not essential to salvation. If it was not necessary it would not be required.

While absolute freedom is absolute nonsense, so is absolute uniformity. We must allow room for honest differences in matters not specifically set out in Scripture.

I hold a high view of Scripture. I believe, as Peter said, "No prophecy of scripture is of any private interpretation [i.e., of private origin]. For the prophecy came not in old time by the will of man; but holy men of God spake as they were moved by the Holy Ghost" (2 Pet 1:20-21).

The word translated "moved" means "to pick up and bear along." It is the picture of a ship with its sails unfurled and being driven through the sea by a mighty wind.

The prophets were not self-starters. They were not original thinkers. They were men upon whom the Holy Spirit came and drove them in their speaking and writing. The divine equation is holy men times the Holy Ghost equals the Holy Bible.

But even if you agreed with me on the essence of Scripture it would not necessarily solve all our differences. We might be equally sincere and devout and equally committed to Scripture and still differ on many issues and emphases. For example, some people are into the "deeper life" while to some of us all that seems like double-talk. We feel we haven't even mastered the "shallow life" yet.

While at a recent meeting of our denomination I boarded a shuttle bus and sat across the aisle from a pastor from one of the New England states. I looked at my bus schedule chart and quipped, "I've got some millennium charts easier to read than this."

And he replied, "Yes, but not nearly as accurate, I'll bet." I agreed and immediately felt a kinship to him.

A few minutes later, however, I heard him tell the person sitting next to him that he had just returned from some nearby atomic testing grounds where he had participated in a peace vigil.

I thought, *I'd never do that.* We could agree on the millennium—the thousand years of peace—but we would not agree on immediate peace. On war and peace, some of us are pacifists, others are nuclear pacifists, and still others defend a just war.

On the sanctity of life, some people argue that all abortions represent murder while others would allow abortions in order to save the life of the mother or in the case of rape and incest.

And we hold differing views on the role of women in the church. Some men and women believe women should not teach or in any way hold authority over men in the church while others would allow them to usher, to be deacons, and still others would allow them to serve as pastors.

What am I saying? Simply this: we must be honest enough and humble enough to admit that we don't know everything and that our opinion is not the final word on every issue. We must not confuse scriptural infallibility with human fallibility. The record of God is perfect, but out understanding of it is not.

In the language of today's teenagers we must give each other some space in those areas where there can be honest differences of interpretation. We must allow for liberty in the nonessentials. That's the Bible way. That's the best way.

Elisabeth Elliot, wife of martyred missionary Jim Elliot, said in her book, *The Liberty of Obedience*, "It appears that God has deliberately left us in a quandary about many things. Why did He not summarize all the rules in one book, and all the basic doctrines in another? He could have eliminated the loopholes, prevented all the schisms over morality and false teaching that have plagued His church for two thousand years. Think of the squabbling and perplexity we would have been spared. And think of the crop of dwarfs he would have reared. He did not spare us because He wants us to reach maturity. He has so arranged things that if we are to go on beyond the 'milk diet' we shall be forced to think."

And, when people think, they come to different conclusions. We must recognize and allow for that. In the nonessentials the law of liberty must prevail.

Love, in Spite of Differences

Finally, the Jerusalem Conference concluded the customs of Jewish believers were to be respected out of Christian love. But they would not coerce. They would appeal to charity and reason. They would trust the Holy Spirit to do His work.

In this we see the third requirement for living together with doctrinal differences. It is, "In all things, charity." If we cannot agree on so many things, how can we be salt and light to the world as Jesus commanded? It is by how we live together and how we love one another in spite of our differences.

My denomination has long been fiercely independent, and at times downright cantankerous. As some wag has put it, "where you have *two* Baptists, you have *three* opinions about everything." And about the only thing two Baptists can agree on is what a third one ought to give. That's close to the truth.

But with all our individuality and independence we must not forget that Jesus said, "By this shall all men know that ye are my disciples, if ye have love one to another" (John 13:35). It is not enough for us to love God and love the lost world. We must also love and accept one another—even when we differ.

It is not necessary for two people to agree on everything in order to work together. Two men can be brothers without being identical twins. We don't have to see eye-to-eye in order to walk arm-in-arm. We can disagree without being disagreeable. We should not fear holding different opinions as long as we do not have an unbrotherly attitude.

We would be wise to give more attention to edifying one another than to classifying one another. We need to ask God to make us mediators, not gladiators. We ought look for common ground, not for a battleground.

John Newton, who wrote great hymns "Amazing Grace" and others, put it all in perspective: "What will it profit a man if he gains his cause, and silences his adversary, if at the same time he loses that humble, tender flame of the Spirit in which the Lord delights, and to which the promise of His presence is made?"

When the city of Constantinople fell to the Turks in the Middle Ages it was reported that while the city was being besieged on the outside, Christian monks on the inside were debating the sex of angels, the color of the eyes of the virgin Mary, and whether a

WORKING OUT DOCTRINAL DIFFERENCES

fly which fell into holy water would be sanctified or the water be polluted.

While these holy men played religious trivia, the city fell to the Moslems. In our day when the world is going to hell at breakneck speed, we must not be found playing religious trivia. We must not major on minors at the expense of our mission. We must live together in peace, in spite of our doctrinal differences.

In the movie, *Lawrence of Arabia*, there is a scene where the English hero of the movie tells his Arab counterpart that if the desert tribes do not unite as a nation, they will be forever destined to be a silly and inconsequential people.

That's what the people of God must do. We must unite or disintegrate into nothingness. But how do we do that?

John Amos Comenius tells us and the early church shows us: "In essentials, unity; in nonessentials, liberty; in all things, charity." That's the secret to living together in peace with doctrinal differences.

9
Bloom Where You Are Planted

When I went to my last church, my boyhood pastor, Dr. John M. Wright, gave me a plaque. The plaque was cut on an angle from a large pine tree so the bark was still around the edges. It was intended to be mounted on a post and placed in a flower bed. The plaque had carved in it the words, "Bloom where you are planted."

I never stuck the sign in the ground, but its message stuck in my mind. It spoke to me: "Put down roots and be faithful and fruitful where you are. Be happy and content where God has placed you."

That's a message ministers and churches need today. Obviously there is much discontent among both of them. Landrum Leavell stated that the average tenure of a Baptist pastor is twenty months. Preachers are like football coaches. They're comers and goers. In many towns preachers are nomads with Bibles, riding through life on a smile, with a shoe shine, and a three-point outline.

Sometimes this discontent is due to the church. A young preacher was being interviewed by a pastor search committee. He asked the chairman of the committee, "Does your church have a deacon rotation plan?" The chairman replied, "Son, around here we rotate pastors."

I heard about a church like that in deep east Texas that changed pastors so often they didn't bother to paint the pastor's name on the church sign. They simply put it on a shingle and hung it with hooks beneath the sign—and, to make matters worse, they didn't paint his name on the shingle—they wrote it in chalk. And, so I am told, the chairman of the deacons sat on the front row during the sermon and tossed an eraser back and forth in his hands.

Sometimes, of course, the problem is the pastor. Preachers sometimes lack the commitment and contentment to stay and work during the dry times and the stormy times. So, when trouble brews, they move on.

But, whatever the reason, we must realize it's difficult to build a church in transit. It's hard to win the world to Christ when you are either loading or unloading a moving van. As one pastor friend expressed it, "If you want to have a successful ministry, set your mailbox in concrete."

Preachers wanting to move is no new phenomenon. It goes all the way back to New Testament times. We catch a hint of this in the words of the apostle Paul to Titus: "For this cause left I thee in Crete, that thou shouldest set in order the things that are wanting, and ordain elders in every city, as I had appointed thee" (Titus 1:5).

The apostle Paul had sent Titus to Crete on a special assignment. His task was twofold, to "set in order" things that were lacking and to "ordain elders" in every church. The phrase "set in order" is a medical term that means "to set in joint." It describes what a doctor does when you go to him with a broken bone. Because the parts of the bone are not in right relationship with one another, the doctor pulls them back into place, so they can heal properly, and the limb can be useful once again.

Situations were not right in the churches of Crete, and Titus had been sent there as a spiritual orthopedist to correct them.

Crete had a reputation for being a hard place. One of their own prophets had said Cretans were "liars, wicked brutes, and lazy gluttons" (v. 12). And, some of that spirit had spilled over into the church. Crete may have been harder than even Paul imagined.

Many scholars believe Titus had written Paul asking to be transferred to a new field. Perhaps he had grown weary in well-doing. Perhaps he felt the Cretans were hopelessly wicked.

Perhaps he felt his life would be happier in Rome or in Athens. But, for whatever reasons, Titus wanted to move.

Paul's response was, "I know Crete is a tough place, but that's why I sent you there. Crete will not be right until the church is right. And the church will not be right unless you stay."

Titus stayed, and today he is the patron saint of the island of Crete.

It has never been easy to pastor a church, but it may be harder today than ever before. If that is so, how can a pastor stay and be happy in today's world? What are the attitudes that will help him find the commitment and contentment to bloom where he is planted?

Young Whippersnappers

First, we need a realistic view of the church. A lot of discontent in the ministry today is due to the illusion on the part of some pastors that out there somewhere is a perfect church where everyone will love them, always follow them, and never criticize them.

I don't want to blunt your idealism, but the church at best is a mixture of the human and the divine. The church is divine because Jesus founded it, indwells it, and He is its head. And as someone said, "One evidence that the church is divine is that it has withstood the ministry for almost 2,000 years."

On the human side, it is comprised of imperfect and immature people. At best, they are in the process of being made perfect, and they are on the road to maturity. But in the meantime, they are awfully human. Until you realize that, you are in for a sad disappointment.

My first pastorate was Belfalls Baptist Church. The little community of Belfalls, Texas, had a cotton gin, a grocery story, a blacksmith shop, a tavern, and the Belfalls Baptist Church that averaged about fifty in Sunday School.

In those days I believed everybody in the church was good, but I soon learned better. Next to the church building was an old tabernacle where summer revival meetings were held. Through the years, time and weather had taken their toll on the tabernacle, and about one third of the shingles were gone from the roof. When the sun shone, the rays of light filtered through. When it rained, the water dripped through, and it had been in that state of disrepair for years.

I thought I was giving dynamic leadership when I said in a sermon one Sunday, "We ought either to repair the tabernacle or tear it down." That seemed reasonable to me.

But, as I greeted the people at the front door following the sermon, one of our elderly deacons said to me, "That's the trouble with our churches today. You young whippersnappers want to tear down everything we older folks have built." As I stood there I had the distinct impression that the church was more apt to replace me than to replace the shingles on that tabernacle.

That's when I first realized people don't always hear what you say, understand what you mean, or agree with your assumptions. And when they disagree, they often strongly oppose you.

When confrontations like that happen, some preachers immediately want to move. But, as my present pastor, Jim Pleitz, quips, "Changing churches is like changing dirty underwear. You are just swapping one set of problems for another." Once you realize that, it will help you to be more content where you are and bloom where you are planted.

Watch Professionalism!

Second, live for the gospel and not for yourself.

One of the most critical concerns we are facing in our churches today is a growing professionalism in the ministry. Too many pastors are driven by selfish ambition. They are caught up in playing the denominational game, seeking prominence, visibility, status, and recognition.

They are insisting upon pastoral authority in a manner that would have shocked our Baptist forebears. They know little of selfless service; they are willing to accept it only as "paying their dues," getting a start in order to move up and out into the limelight.

I find it strange that many pastors who claim to be followers of the One who "made himself of no reputation" (Phil. 2:7) are so busy trying to build their own.

If I understand the Bible, a pastor has three duties. He is to *lead the sheep, feed the sheep,* and *bleed for the sheep.* Jesus said, "The good shepherd lays down his life for the sheep" (John 10:11, NIV). He is the chief Shepherd, and we are His undershepherds (1 Pet. 5:4). As He laid down His life in substitution for the sheep, so we must be willing to lay ours down in service and ministry for them.

There is so little of that today. One of the saddest comments I have heard recently was a lady saying, concerning her pastor, "That man doesn't serve our church. It serves him."

Following the last supper, Jesus, girding Himself with a towel, took a basin of water, and washed His disciples' feet. In so doing He was assuming the role of a servant. When He finished He said, "Ye call me Master and Lord: and ye say well; for so I am. If I then, your Lord and Master, have washed your feet; you also ought to wash one another's feet. For I have given you an example, that you should do as I have done to you" (John 13:13-15).

This is the only time, so far as we know, that Jesus said He had given us an example—and it was on the occasion when He humbled Himself to become a servant of others.

If He, our Lord and Master, stooped to assume the role of a servant, so should we. It is clear to me, the symbol of the pastor's office is washing feet, not whipping the saints.

Jesus concluded this teaching by saying, "If you know these things, happy are ye if you do them." The joy of the ministry is found in serving.

Much discontent among pastors today is due to the fact that we sometimes try to build our own kingdom instead of His kingdom. Then, when things do not work out to our advantage or our advancement, we get discouraged.

Paul wrote the Book of Philippians from prison in Rome. The church at Philippi was greatly concerned about his physical and emotional well-being and kept up communications with him. Imprisonment would most certainly curtail his missionary activities and thus dampen his enthusiasm. They were concerned how it would affect his spirit.

Paul was emphatic, "I would ye should understand, brethren, that the things which happened unto me have fallen out rather unto the furtherance of the gospel" (1:12). Then he explained how as a result of his imprisonment the gospel was going to places it otherwise would not have gone and other Christians were being inspired by his courage.

The word "furtherance" describes the action of a band of woodcutters who preceded the regular army in the first century to cut away the underbrush and allow the army to make a swift advance. Paul said, in essence, that his imprisonment had actually led to a pioneer advance of the gospel by carrying it into places it otherwise would not have gone and inspiring people who otherwise would have become discouraged.

Paul "bloomed where he was planted" because he was living for the gospel and not for himself. If the gospel was going well, it did not matter what happened to him.

Jesus said, "Whosoever will save his life shall lose it; but whosoever loses his life for my sake and the gospel's, the same shall save it" (Mark 8:35). The more we live for ourselves, the less we find joy and contentment in life. The more we lose ourselves in the cause of Christ and for the sake of the gospel, the more readily we find peace and contentment. It is only as we live for the gospel and not for ourselves that we can really bloom where we are planted.

Watch Out for Acid

Third, don't harbor bitterness and resentment in your heart. One of the leading characters in a popular television series, speaking of his up-and-down love life, said. "I've been burnt so many times I need to carry a fire extinguisher." Anyone who has pastored for a reasonable period of time knows what it is to be burnt.

People say things and do things, sometimes intentionally, sometimes unintentionally, that hurt us. And, they hurt us deeply. If we aren't careful, we will allow those hurts to canker into bitterness and resentment.

I was considering a move to another church several years ago and word leaked out about it. I received this anonymous note from one of our members:

> This note is frank. Everyone knows about the offer you are considering. Why don't you take it and leave Green Acres! We need a change.... We need a new pastor who can put us at the top and out front as a community leader... We love you—but we don't need you anymore.... A concerned, but loving member.

That will bless you, won't it? With friends like that, who needs enemies?

When I received that letter, Green Acres was twice as big as any other church in East Texas and the sixth largest church in all of Texas.

During my years as pastor we had grown from an average attendance of 700 in Sunday School to an average of 2,500 per Sunday and were still growing. We were $30,000 ahead of our budget in the midst of the worst recession Texas had experienced since the Great Depression.

We were sponsoring five local missions and had averaged building a church in a foreign country every year for eleven years. We were debt free and averaging sixteen new members per Sunday as we had for sixteen years.

And my friend wanted strong leadership to put Green Acres "at the top and out front." It's not easy to keep a sweet spirit in times like that.

But, every leader should expect that some people will not like him—and that they will say so. But it still hurts. After pastoring for thirty-five years I think I understand why Frederick the Great said, "The more I know people, the more I like my dog."

And, that quote might have inspired former President Harry S. Truman to say, "If you want a friend in Washington, get you a dog."

But, no matter how hurting or unjustified it may be, we must not harbor anger and bitterness. Someone has said, "Anger and bitterness are like acid. They do more damage to the vessel in which they are stored than to the object on which they are poured."

The Bible gives us the tragic example of a man who lost his joy and contentment because of hatred and anger. Haman was the crown prince of Persia in the days of Esther. He had everything a person could want in life—position, power, wealth, and prominence. But he also had an intense hatred for a Jew named Mordecai. One day as he recounted all of the blessings and benefits of his life, he said, "Yet all of this availeth me nothing, so long as I see Mordecai, the Jew, sitting at the king's gate" (Esth. 5:13).

His hatred was so immense that it kept him from enjoying his blessings. You know "the rest of the story," to quote Paul Harvey. Haman was hanged on the gallows he had built for Mordecai. Bitterness and anger can do the same to us. They can rob us of the contentment that prevents us from blooming where we are planted.

Don't Become Their Project

Fourth, you should keep challenging goals before your people. Many pastors are unhappy and discontent because they are not going anywhere and they are not doing anything. They just rock along until they move on. They have no real goals. This can be devastating.

Buzz Aldren, the second man to walk on the moon, came back to the earth and had a nervous breakdown. He explained his predicament in part by saying, "When you have achieved all your goals, depression sets in."

Do you know what the goal of most churches is? It is to meet next Sunday. Then when they meet next Sunday, they immediately set a new goal—to meet the next Sunday. Their only goal is to meet. And, they are always achieving it. Beyond that they have no grand purpose or scheme. Is there little wonder there is so much unhappiness in the ministry today?

What is a worthy goal for a church? It should be to get the maximum yield from your field. Church fields, like agricultural fields, are not all equally productive. Some soil is rich and fertile. Other soil is bleak and barren.

It is the same with church fields. The Lord doesn't expect every pastor to build a big church. Not all fields have that kind of potential. But the Lord expects us to be faithful and diligent. He expects you to get the maximum yield out of your field.

Beyond this general goal you need to have some specific goals. You need to know the number of people you hope to reach, the number of missions you want to establish, the number of ministries you plan to begin and you need to hold these goals before your people.

Tim LaHaye, in his book, *If Ministers Fall, Can They Be Restored?* tells of a favorite uncle who had pastored for fifty-five years. His uncle said to him on one occasion, "Son, always keep a project before your people. Otherwise, you will become their project."

Keeping challenging goals before you and your congregation is the secret to contentment for both the pastor and the people.

Watch Your Complaining

Fifth, you should keep an attitude of gratitude. The writings of the apostle Paul are filled with expressions of gratitude on his part. He is grateful for his salvation, for his selection into God's service, and even for his suffering (Phil. 1:29).

Modern ministers need to discover and cultivate this same attitude of gratitude—both to God and His people. The leader of the Coptic Church said, "If you carry the cross of Christ on your shoulder, you should do so without complaint."

Sometimes some of the most whining, complaining people on earth are ministers. The Bible describes Christians as soldiers.

BLOOM WHERE YOU ARE PLANTED

And it says we are engaged in a spiritual warfare. Soldiers, in a time of war, should expect hardships. And, they should expect that some of them will be wounded and that others will die. So when those things happen they are not surprised. They expect them.

As soldiers of the cross we expect some casualties also. And we accept that without complaint.

Rejoice in Your Relationship

Sixth, you should find joy in your relationship with Christ, not in your success. The gospel of Luke tells of Jesus sending the seventy out on a great evangelistic mission. They came back elated over the fact that the demons were subject unto them. Jesus warned, "Rejoice not that the spirits are subject unto you; but rather rejoice, because your names are written in heaven" (Luke 10:20).

What did Jesus mean by that? He meant they should not rejoice in their success, but in their relationship. He knew the time would come when they would go out and the demons would not be subject to them. What would they do then? Where would their joy be then? So, he warned, "Don't rejoice in your success; rejoice in your relationship that your names are written in heaven."

Victories are temporal. Our relationship to Christ is eternal. Success is passing. Salvation is permanent.

If you find or seek joy in success you are destined to disappointment. All churches plateau sooner or later—and I do mean all.

Deepen Your Ministry—Let God Broaden It

Seventh, you should trust your ministry to the Lord and not to men. I had to make that choice early in my life. I was serving on the board of trustees for one of our Baptist institutions when there came a division on our board over several unethical practices involving the administrator. Some of us tried to resolve the matter quietly but we were not able to do so because the administrator would not cooperate. The only course left was to take the matter to the full board for its review and action. The lines were soon rigidly drawn between us. I was a young pastor and took a very strong stand.

In the weeks prior to that meeting we busied ourselves getting the facts of the issue. Several influential people on the board were close personal friends to the administrator. They were committed to protecting him no matter what. So, while we spent our time gathering acts, they spent their time getting votes. When the full board came together their first item of business was to vote not to hear our facts. Naturally, my side lost decisively.

Following that meeting, another trustee, a prominent layman who was on the opposite side of the issue, asked me to have lunch with him. After the meal he said, "Paul, you are a fine young preacher with a promising future. But, if you don't change your ways I will see to it that you never go anywhere in this state."

I thanked him for his advice, but right there I determined I would trust my ministry to the Lord and not to men. I would work at pastoring my people, winning the lost, preparing and preaching sermons, doing the things the Lord called me to do, and let Him take care of me.

Thereafter, I served when asked but never sought any position. I did what God called me to do and trusted my ministry and future to Him. He has proved more than trustworthy.

Years later I heard a minister say, "You deepen your ministry and let God broaden it." That's my advice to you. Bloom where you are planted. Put down roots where God has placed you. Be faithful and fruitful in the field He has given to you. Then, if He has a wider ministry for you, He will bring it to pass.

Martin Luther was threatened by a representative of the Pope. The messenger reminded Luther of the papal power and warned him of the day when he would be deserted by his supporters. "Where will you be then?" Luther was asked. He responded, "Then, as now, in the hands of Almighty God!" That's the safest place for any of us to be.

BLOOM WHERE YOU ARE PLANTED

I was in a Bible conference with Herschel Hobbs several years ago when he told me about his brother-in-law, now deceased. While the man was in college he went to one of his professors and asked, "I want to move to a new church. Would you help me?" The professor responded, "Now, Henry, you make a fire where you are and someone will see your smoke and come over to see what it's about."

That's good advice. If you want to move, send up a smoke signal. Build a fire where you are. People will notice it in time.

The movie, *Glory*, is about the Massachusetts 54th Army, the first black battalion in the Civil War. Their first battle was against insurmountable odds. The night before they had a prayer meeting around the campfire. The sergeant prayed, "Lord, if we die, let the word go back to our friends that we went down standing up."

That's the way I feel. I don't want to come to the end of my ministry whipped, whining, and washed out. I want to go down standing up. I want to "bloom where I'm planted." Don't you?

10
Shake the Dust from Your Feet

An unemployed preacher said to a friend, "I can tell you one thing, I ain't no quitter. I pastored three churches and stayed with all three till they died."

It is possible to stay in a place too long. Jesus made it clear that there is a time to go when He told His disciples to "shake off the dust of your feet" (Matt. 10:14).

These words were part of Jesus' instructions to the Twelve as He sent them out on their first preaching mission. In preparation for this new ministry He told them where to go, what to say, what to take, how to act, what to expect, and how to deal with rejection.

Jesus' statement "shake off the dust of your feet" was a part of His advice on how to deal with rejection. Our Lord Himself had already been rejected at Nazareth and in the country of the Gadarenes and was rejected afterwards at a Samaritan village. Indeed, in general, "He came unto his own, and his own received him not" (John 1:11). These disciples needed to be prepared for the same kind of response from some people.

Shaking the dust from one's feet was a Jewish practice when leaving Gentile soil. To a Jew the dust of a Gentile place was defiling. Therefore, when a Jew crossed the border of Palestine and entered into his own country after a journey into Gentile lands, he shook the dust of the Gentile road off his feet, that the last particle of pollution might be cleansed away. So Jesus said, "If a city or a village will not receive you, you must treat it like a Gentile place." You are to shake the dust of that place off your feet and to move on. He is saying there is a time to seek a new place and a new opportunity.

The apostles took this saying of Jesus literally and when the Jews of Antioch rejected their message Paul and Barnabas shook the dust from their feet and moved on to Iconium (Acts 13:51).

There is a principle here for the modern-day minister. It is possible to stay too long. There is a time to go. There are times when you need, so to speak, to shake the dust of where you are from your feet and move to a new place and a new people. But, when is that? How do we know when to move?

There are at least five times when a person, I think, needs to move.

You Only Have So Many Ideas

First, you need to move on when you lose your vision. Let's face it, one person has just so many ideas, just so many dreams. One person can be only so creative. And when he reaches his limit he needs to move on and make a fresh start. This is especially true in the earlier years of a pastor's ministry. With time and experience he may be able to come up with enough dreams and fresh ideas to keep a growing congregation challenged, but it is no easy task. To stay in one place a long time and keep a vibrant work going, especially when you are young, requires more creativity than most people are capable of.

Several years ago I read an article in the *Houston Post* about former Texas governor John Connelly that underscores what I am saying. He was living in Houston at the time and leading the political campaign of a mayoral candidate.

Connelly freely admitted that Houston had been blessed with good visionary leaders throughout most of its history and he even acknowledged that the incumbent mayor, Kathy Whitmire, whom his candidate was opposing, had done an outstanding job. "Why, then, did he want to unseat her?" he was asked.

He responded, "I'm not going to be critical of her, but she has been mayor for eight years and basically I think that is long enough. It is time for new leadership."

Then he added, "I left the governor's office after six years even though I think I could have been elected for a fourth term." "But," he said, "you can't be there forever. You can't solve all the problems. And the time comes when you ought to move on. Each person has just so much to give in terms of imagination, drive, energy, and once a person has served so long, he spends more time defending his record than coming up with solutions."

Not long after that I heard a news commentary on West German chancellor Helmut Kohl that suggested the same thing. For years Helmut Kohl had been an immensely popular politician. And during the preceding year he had managed the political unification of Germany masterfully. But now he was in trouble politically and he wanted an endorsement from President Bush to bolster his chances of reelection.

Why was he in trouble? One analyst put it succinctly, "He simply ran out of ideas."

We all do eventually.

I picked up a newspaper in San Francisco that carried the front page story about the death of Henry Ford II, grandson of the founder of Ford Motor Company. *Automotive News* had acclaimed Ford as "the last of the great American industrial czars."

It is generally agreed that if Henry Ford had not taken over the Ford Motor Company in 1945 there would be no Ford Motor Company today. For, at that time, the company was losing $1 million a day. But, with his drive, energy, and determination he brought Ford from the brink of disaster into its golden era. However, Robert Lacy wrote, Ford apparently stayed too long. "In the closing days of his leadership," Lacy said, "much of his energy went into not making mistakes. And the longer he ran it, the more conservative the Ford Motor Company became."

When I read that article it reminded me of his grandfather Henry Ford, who founded the Ford Motor Company in 1901. Old Henry was an inspired tinkerer, an American original, a truly great industrialist, who put the world on wheels.

SHAKE THE DUST FROM YOUR FEET

He incorporated the Ford Motor Company in 1903. In 1908 he produced his first Model T automobile. In 1914 he began paying his workers the unheard of wage of $5 a day so they could afford to buy his automobile. And he invented the world's first moving assembly line.

But with all his creative genius Ford made one fatal mistake. According to his biographer, Robert Lacy, Ford "developed a fixation with his masterpiece which was almost unhealthy." In spite of the fact that General Motors was capturing more and more of the market at Ford's expense, he refused to consider updating or replacing the Model T until he was driven to do so.

These are dangers we all face if we stay too long—spending our energies trying not to make a mistake and developing such a fixation on the past that we are unwilling to change in the present. That's why when you run out of ideas, or you lose your vision, it's time to move on.

Leadership Doesn't Come on Credit

Another time when you need to move is when you have lost your leadership. That can happen in many ways. Moses lost his leadership because of pride. Rehoboam lost his leadership because he refused to listen to wise counsel. Solomon lost his leadership because of greed. And Samson lost his leadership because of sexual sins.

Through conflict, through mistakes, through sin, through angering enough people or the wrong people, through bad decisions or wrong behavior, and through foolish fights the modern leader can do the same thing. He can forfeit his leadership. He can put himself on the shelf.

Leadership isn't automatic and it's not forever. It has to be earned. It comes by hard work, a loving spirit, wise decisions, a godly life—and time. But, just as surely as it is earned it can be lost.

A. W. Tozer, speaking to a group of ministers, said it best, "It is possible for a man to run against the wrong object and bend his lance for good." So by foolish conflicts, unwise choices, and wrong priorities a minister can forfeit his opportunity and usefulness.

Someone asked Chuck Colson what he thought were the most important characteristics of a Christian leader. He replied, "That's easy. Integrity! Integrity! Integrity!"

Integrity is the glue that holds life and leadership together for the minister. If he loses that, he's dead in the water.

In his book, *The Eagle and the Raven*, James A. Michener (State House Press, Austin, Texas, 1990, 209) contrasts General Sam Houston and General Santa Anna as leaders. In the last paragraph of the last chapter of the book he writes,

> Eagle and Raven! They were not ordinary men, and never in their long lives did they behave in ordinary ways. Similar in much, they differed in one crucial dimension. Houston had a heart of oak, forever loyal to the principles to which he had been bred and upon which he had nurtured during his embattled career. Santa Anna was a bending willow, subservient to every story, elegant and daring, but never faithful to any principle, not even those of his own devising. A national leader may accumulate a spectacular chain of temporary results, but unless his character has been forged in the fires of integrity and his actions in the crucible of hard-edged reason, history will refuse to stamp him with the seal of greatness.

The wise pastor will guard his character carefully for once his credibility is lost his leadership is lost. And when that happens it's time to move.

Watch the Bucket Committee!

Third, you need to move on when you determine the people do not want to do anything. There are some churches that are at ease in Zion. They are content with business as usual. Their motto is "Nothing Ventured, Nothing Lost." And their theme song is, "We Will Not Be Moved." They have already put out the "Please Do Not Disturb" sign.

An unknown but insightful poet spoke of some churches when he wrote:

> Our fathers have been churchmen
> For a hundred years or so
> And to every new proposal
> Their response is always, "No."

A fellow pastor who had just resigned his church with no place to go, said to me, "I really stayed too long. The church was on the decline when I went there. I thought I could turn it around in two years but I didn't take into account the mind-set of the people. They are good people but not big thinkers. They are not progressive."

You have only one life to live. You have only so much energy to give. You have only so long to serve. Once you determine a people don't want to do anything and won't be led, move on. Don't waste your life on people who have determined to do nothing.

But a word of caution is in order, there will be some resistance to leadership in every church. Expect it! Don't be thrown by it! A pastor friend told me he had a "bucket committee" in his church. I thought I had heard of every committee in captivity, but that was a new one on me. So I said to him, "I have thirty-eight standing committees, two sitting committees, three lying committees, and one dead committee. But I don't have a bucket committee."

He replied, "Yes, you do. It's a self-appointed, standing committee. It's always at work. When the preacher gets fired up they pour cold water on him."

I said, "Man, I not only have that committee, I know who the chairman is."

There is a bucket committee in every church. But don't mistake a little opposition for a hardened resistance to leadership. And remember, too, that most people need a leader to get anything done. That's why God put you there. Nonetheless, if you determine the people will not be led, move on to people who will be.

That's really the idea behind Jesus' statement, "Shake off the dust of your feet." If you encounter people who are determined to reject you and the truth when it is presented to them, then move on to a more responsive people.

A Tip from the Golf Pro

Fourth, you need to move when you receive a higher calling. My decision to accept the presidency of the Annuity Board of the Southern Baptist Convention was the most difficult decision of my life. It came when I was 55 years of age and happily situated in the pastorate.

I had an excellent staff, a loving congregation, a host of friends, and a record of seventeen years of growth. And I had just led my church to adopt a challenging ten-year plan of progress and growth that would carry me through to retirement. I had everything a pastor could ask for. I fully intended to stay at my present church the rest of my life.

When the call came from the Annuity Board it was disruptive to say the least. I prayed about it, talked with my wife about it, counseled with my friends about it, and prayed some more. Nothing seemed to help. The crossroads of decision is always a lonely place. You must stand there alone. So, the Lord and I grappled with this life-changing decision.

The Annuity Board's quarterly trustee meeting was approaching and I had to make a decision. From the airport in Tyler I called ahead to tell the chairman of the committee that my answer was no. I was going to stay as pastor at Green Acres.

He urged me to pray about it on the flight to New Orleans. I always pray on planes. I sit lightly in the seat, hold my feet off the floor, and pray and pray and pray.

When I reached New Orleans my answer was the same, "No." The committee asked me to reconsider. So I prayed as I have never prayed before. Still, no clear answer came.

One day I was at the Westwood Driving Range in Tyler, trying to relax, but the decision still weighed heavily on my mind. Ophel Caldwell, the golf pro at the driving range, was a part of our church's television audience and a special friend. I shared with him my dilemma and his immediate response was, "A higher calling. That's what you've got. A higher calling."

The next few days, his words kept ringing in my ears, "A

higher calling... a higher calling." I couldn't get them out of my mind.

A few days later a friend asked, "How do you feel now that you've made your big decision?" I responded, almost without thinking, "Miserable! I feel miserable!"

I left my friend and called the chairman of the Annuity Board search committee and told him if they still wanted me I was willing to come.

A higher calling is not necessarily to a bigger place, but it is to a more challenging place, a more demanding place, a place where you are more needed at that time.

The apostle Paul spoke of pressing "toward the mark for the prize of the high calling of God" (Phil. 3:14). That's what I had.

When you receive a higher calling you need to go.

Grow Old Along with Me

Finally, you need to move when you reach retirement age. One of the most prominent and successful pastors in our Convention said, "There is no record in history of a church continuing to grow after its pastor reaches sixty-five." Though he stayed much beyond that, I still think he was right. The reasons are many. For one thing the church as a whole begins to anticipate the pastor's retirement and is not apt to launch out on bold new projects. They are far more likely to coast than to gear up. For another, the people, especially the young people, are ready for new leadership. And, too, about that age most men lose much of their stamina and simply cannot keep the pace they once kept.

Some pastors rationalize staying beyond their retirement years thinking, *My people want me to stay.* No. What they mean is, "My friends want me to stay." If they took a survey of their entire church they would discover that many people, especially the younger people, are ready for a new leader. Their friends simply tell them what they want to hear and their enemies don't tell them anything.

Others do not retire when they should because they cannot

afford to. They have not made adequate financial preparation for retirement and stay at the church much longer than they should for economic reasons. They stay because they cannot afford to leave.

The bottom line is, there is a time to stay and a time to leave. Wise is the pastor who knows when to step down and move on.

11
Working with Other Denominations

Denominationalism has been the characteristic expression of Christianity on the ecclesiastical side since the Reformation. In the beginning days of Christianity there were no denominations. All believers were one. In those days, the followers of Christ were called by many names. They were called believers, brethren, disciples, saints, and servants. And, finally, in Antioch for the first time, they were called Christians.

They were called believers for their faith; brothers for their love; disciples for their knowledge; saints for their holiness; servants for their work; and Christians for their Lord.

During the first 300 years the church flourished in spite of great persecution as an illegal religion. Then in A.D. 312 Constantine, emperor of the Roman Empire, was converted to Christianity. So the story goes, the night before a great battle he had a vision in which he saw a cross and heard a voice saying, "By this sign conquer." As a result of this experience he embraced Christianity.

Constantine was the first emperor of the Roman Empire to profess Christianity. Under him the church was recognized as a legal body and became the official religion of the Roman Empire. Moreover, he gave many gifts to the church including huge estates, and he built the first great Christian cathedral.

Whereas Christianity had flourished under persecution, now with the favor and fortune of government, it began to decline. Heresy, worldliness, and paganism slowly crept in.

Gradually there was a blending of the powers of the church and the powers of the state until the church held both political and ecclesiastical power. And it used those powers to suppress, control, and persecute those who did not agree with it. So, for 1,000 years there was only one church.

These were the dark ages of church history. True Christianity all but disappeared from the face of the earth. If the pure and simple faith of Jesus was alive during those years, it was underground, suppressed and hidden.

In 1508-1509 a monk by the name of Martin Luther, while studying the Bible, concluded that God's favor is not a prize to be won, but a gift to be accepted. He rediscovered the simple biblical truth that it is only when a man has stopped trying to achieve God's favor by his own abilities and accomplishments that he can understand and receive the grace of God.

Luther tried to reform the Roman Catholic Church. Hence his movement was called the Reformation. But, being unable to do so he was forced to break with it. His followers became known as Lutherans. He was able to survive prison, attempts on his life, and persecution from the established church only because of the rising tide of democracy in Europe due to the disintegration of the Holy Roman Empire.

It was also about this same time that the printing press was invented. Now, for the first time, the common man had both increased freedom and the Scriptures in his own language.

The kind of liberty that Luther claimed for himself soon spread throughout all of Europe. The right to private judgment and freedom from ecclesiastical superiors led to a great variety of interpretations of the New Testament. It was out of this climate that denominationalism was born.

A denomination, by definition, is a group of congregations who share the same name, the same basic beliefs, and who exchange pastors and members.

Today, according to researcher David Barrett, there is a pluralism and a proliferation of 22,800 denominations worldwide. My folks, Baptists, are but one of them, and there are at least fifty different kinds of Baptists in the United States alone.

It is my view that all denominations are man-made, even those

WORKING WITH OTHER DENOMINATIONS

who say they aren't. By this I mean they all grew out of human interpretations of Scripture, and their beginnings can all be traced back to a time and place in history. They all began with a human leader or a group who held a particular interpretation of Scripture. Around that individual or that group sprang up other bodies who shared the same beliefs.

Thus, Lutherans, Presbyterians, Episcopalians, Methodists, and Baptists came into being. Other groups, such as the Nazarenes, Church of Christ, and Disciples of Christ were offshoots of these older denominations.

Denominationalism is not all bad. At its best it simply means there are things Christians disagree on that are important. It says, "I have certain convictions I feel strongly about." As soon as people begin to grow in their faith they develop certain convictions. For example, Christians disagree on whether infants should be baptized or whether baptism should be reserved for believers only. Differences like these become fertile soil out of which denominations grow.

On the downside, denominationalism has done immeasurable harm to the cause of Christ. As John R. Mott, one of the founders of the YMCA movement, once said, "The price that has been paid for a divided Christendom is an unbelieving world." It has led to bitter rivalry and intense competition. The result has been confusion and conflict in the family of God.

Christians should not be asked to set aside their convictions, but since we are all touched by sin and none of us have the final word from God, we should hold onto our convictions firmly with one hand and extend our other hand in love and acceptance to people who disagree with us. We need to realize that a person can be wrong on some issues and still be a part of the Christian family.

Denominational rivalry and narrow sectarianism that lead us to think the blessings of God cannot come on any group but ours, to believe that our way is the only way and to feel that unless people are a part of us, they do not belong to Him, is wrong.

Jesus issued a stinging rebuke on this kind of rivalry and

prejudice one day when he was teaching His disciples about true greatness. He said to them, "Whosoever shall receive [a little child] in my name, receiveth me; And whosoever shall receive me receiveth not me, but him that sent me" (Mark 9:37).

That phrase, "in my name," must have struck home with John for it brought to his mind an experience which he and James had in Galilee. They had seen an exorcist casting a devil out of a man "in Jesus' name" and they had tried to stop him. John doesn't try to cover up why. The reason he gave was "he followed not us" (v. 38).

This unknown exorcist was obviously sincere and successful. He was not attempting to cast a devil out. He was doing it. And, he was not doing it by any of the incantations of the heathen, but in Jesus' name.

But the man was without apostolic commission for doing this. He was irregular, he was not of the true order. He was not in the appointed succession. He was an outsider.

John's statement revealed a jealous and exclusive spirit unworthy of the ministry of Christ. He had a deep prejudice and an unwillingness to accept anyone except those of his own circle. He expressed the narrowest kind of sectarianism.

Jesus' reply was quick, sharp, and stern. Like a clap of thunder follows a blaze of lightning came the Lord's words, "[Don't hinder him.] He that is not against us is on our part" (vv. 39-40).

Jesus did not quibble about details. If the man was using His name in a sincere desire to help others, he ought not to be stopped. If lives are being blessed and delivered from the power of evil, such work ought not to be hindered.

There is no more forthright rebuke of denominational narrowness or ecclesiastical intolerance than this. This man was doing the Master's work, in the Master's name, by the Master's power and should not be hindered. He ought rather to be esteemed as a friend and a helper, not treated as an enemy. A jealous and exclusive spirit is unworthy of the minister of Christ.

The lesson of tolerance that is so needed today is taught here. We sadly err if we feel that spiritual blessings cannot come through any church other than the one with which we are affiliated. God does not empty His fullness into one mold.

The text then is a plea that we take a wide view of our faith instead of a narrow one. The followers of Jesus are not to be a little clique over in a corner. Those who do the work of Jesus belong to Him.

So, Jesus was saying in part, "Do not look for labels, look for fruit—the activities, attitudes, and Spirit of Christ. When you find it, rejoice and encourage it. Don't meet it with sour, skeptical antagonism. And don't be in conflict with My followers just because they are not a part of your group." In these words our Master laid down a principle of love and acceptance of those "not in our group" for His disciples for all time.

Don't be misled by the statement of Jesus, "[The man who] is not against us is on our part." It does not teach that anything goes or that neutrality toward Christ is acceptable. It must be balanced with Christ's complementary expression, "He that is not with me is against me, and he that gathereth not is with me scattereth abroad," found in Matthew 12:30. The person who refuses to take his stand with Christ is against Christ. The person who takes a stand with Christ and is doing His work, however imperfectly, is not against Him.

This is a plea for tolerance and charity. It does not mean that we are to accept false teachings and heresy. But remember, this man was doing the Master's work in the Master's name, by the Master's power. And wherever we find that we are to encourage it.

One of the chief values of this experience is that it provides for us the bottom-line tests of real Christianity, and the marks of a true church. What are they? Like the man who was casting out demons, they must be doing the Master's work, in the Master's name, by the Master's power. Wherever we find that being done we are to encourage it and support it, not hinder it. With this criteria let us examine ourselves as well as others.

Sleeping Giants

First the true church is one that does the Master's work. What is the Master's work? In the broadest sense, it is helping people in Jesus' name. In the verse preceding this text Jesus said, "Whosoever shall receive one of such children in my name, receiveth me" (v. 37). In the verse following this text Jesus said, "Whosoever shall give you a cup of water to drink in my name, because ye belong to Christ, verily I say unto you, he shall not lose his reward" (v. 41). In other places Jesus talked about giving food to the hungry, clothes to the naked, water to the thirsty, friendship to the lonely, encouragement to the wayward, and hope to the sick. In each instance he said, "Inasmuch as ye have done it unto one of the least of these my brethren, ye have done it unto me" (Matt. 25:40). It is clear in Scripture, we serve the Master by serving other people.

In the strictest sense, the work of the Master is to set people free from the bondage of sin and Satan. In this instance, the unknown exorcist was casting devils out of people. He was setting them free from the grip of evil. That is always the primary work of the church.

So, the real test of God's work is, "Are lives being changed? Are homes being saved? Are people being helped? Are people being delivered? Are they being set free?" The true church is not a yachting club but a fishing fleet. There is a difference in the two. A yachting club is made up of the rich and idle who go to their club to enjoy and impress one another and to spend their leisure time. A fishing fleet is made up of workers engaged in a meaningful pursuit.

As the people of God, we are here to rescue the perishing and care for the dying. We must never be content to sit and sing "Just As I Am" to one another. We are to be fishers of men.

The most tragic war in American history was the Civil War fought 1861-1865. In that war we not only lost more American lives than in any other war, more Americans were lost than in all other wars put together. The four years of bloodshed left a

WORKING WITH OTHER DENOMINATIONS

heritage of grief and bitterness that remains in part even unto today.

One of the tragedies of the Civil War is that it lasted far longer than it had to if the Union army had not had such incompetent generals. The Union forces were far larger than those of the Confederacy. In the last years of the war the North had more than one million men in arms. The South probably had no more than 200,000. But, the Union army had a succession of inept generals—George B. McClellan, Ambrose E. Burnside, Joseph Hooker, and George G. Meade. President Lincoln once said of McClellan, his first general, "There is no doubt little Mac has a permanent case of the slumbers."

Many churches and many Christians today are like General McClellan—they have a permanent case of the slumbers. They are sound asleep. They are giants—sleeping giants. They need to wake up and get on with the work of God.

I was in an evangelistic meeting recently where the leader kept exhorting the people to pray for a fresh moving of God in their midst. It occurred to me that we are often praying for a fresh moving of God when we are the ones who need to get moving.

Many churches are suffering from the paralysis of analysis. They are analyzing and organizing when they need to be agonizing and evangelizing. Without realizing it, they have become one of God's frozen chosen—cold, stiff, and indifferent.

Someone asked Mother Teresa if she thought she would ever go to the moon. She replied, "if there are people there I am sure my sisters and I would go." That's the spirit we need. And wherever we find people doing the Master's work we should encourage them, not criticize them, and oppose them.

The Cassava of Life

Second, the true church is one that does the Master's work in the Master's name. Three times in this passage and the verses surrounding it you will find the statement, "In my name." Jesus spoke of receiving a little child "in my name," of casting out demons "in my name," and of giving a cup of water "in my name."

Jesus is the center and the circumference of our faith. All that we are and do depends upon Him. He is the Alpha and the Omega—and all the letters in between. He is the door. Apart from Him we do not enter in. And He is the Bread of life.

A missionary friend from Africa told of a native who came to her once and asked that she explain the meaning of Jesus' statement, "I am the Bread of life." The reason for his difficulty in understanding that verse was that in the bush country they do not have bread to eat. Only the wealthy people in the city could afford bread. He therefore associated bread with people who are rich.

She then asked him what the staple food of the bush was—the food everyone ate. He told her it was cassava. Cassava is a white root that can be boiled and eaten like a baked sweet potato or ground up and eaten like grits. It is the staple of the natives' diet.

She then said, "Read the verse and in the place of bread insert the word *cassava*." He then read the verse, "I am the cassava of life." A smile came across his face and he exclaimed, "Oh, now I understand."

Jesus is the Bread of life. All the vitamins and calories your soul requires are in Him.

A test then of a true church is: Is it working "in Jesus' name?" Is He the centerpiece of all we do? We can do much good in the name of humanity, in the name of charity, in the name of brotherhood, or in our own name. But if we are the true people of God, what we do must be in His name.

One Sunday night at the close of the evening worship service I had the children of the church I pastored come to the front of the sanctuary for a visit with the pastor. After interviewing those who had a birthday that week I called on a little girl to pray. She prayed, "Lord, we thank you for Jesus, God's only forgotten Son."

In many churches today Jesus is all but forgotten. God's only begotten Son has become God's forgotten Son. When that happens, the group ceases to be a church regardless of what it is called. But when we encounter people doing the Master's work in the Master's name, we should befriend them and not fight them.

Watch Out for Ghosts

Third, the true church is one that does the Master's work, in the Master's name, by the Master's power. What do you know about the Holy Spirit? My earliest recollections of church have to do with Him. The first seven years of my life I lived in the little east Texas sawmill town of Wiergate. Down the sandy lane from our house was a little white frame Methodist Church. We had to walk past it to go almost anyplace—to town, to the swimming pool, to the movie theater, and to the homes of most of our friends.

My family never attended church. My dad, in fact, had a hostile attitude toward preachers and churches and delighted in ridiculing them and making fun of them. The first remembrance I have of church is his telling my sister and me that a ghost (the Holy Ghost) lived in that church house. Thereafter, and until I learned better, every time I walked past the church alone I would get as far across the sandy road as possible and walk sideways with my face to the church and my back to the picket fence that lined the street. I was watching for ghosts.

There are a lot of people today who are about as ignorant of the Holy Spirit as I was. They know His name, but they do not know who he is or what He does. And, because they do not know Him, they are afraid of Him.

Christians and churches do not need to be afraid of the Holy Spirit. We need rather to make friends with Him and draw upon Him for it is by His power that we live and serve (Acts 1:8).

Wherever He is at work, supernatural things happen. So we need to ask ourselves of our own work and that of others, "Is there anything happening here that cannot be explained by human organization or manipulation? Is there anything taking place that cannot be accounted for and explained by our own efforts? Is there a demonstration of the power of God here?"

A. W. Tozer said, "If the Holy Spirit was withdrawn from the church today, 95 percent of what we do would go on, and no one would know the difference. If the Holy Spirit had been withdrawn from the New Testament church, 95 percent of what they did would have stopped, and everybody would have known the difference."

There was in this man's ministry the evident work of God and there ought to be in ours also.

Carl Bates, former president of the Southern Baptist Convention, once said: "There came a time in my life when I earnestly prayed, 'God, I want more power.' Time wore on and the power did not come. One day the burden was more than I could bear. I asked, 'God, why haven't you answered that prayer?' God seemed to whisper back His simple reply, 'With plans no bigger than yours, you don't need My power.'"

The Master's work, in the Master's name, and by the Master's power—that's what we are to be about. Wherever that takes place we are to rejoice in it not hinder it. The person or church doing that is our ally, not our enemy, whether they belong to our group or not.

This chapter, then, is a plea for less conflict and competition between denominations. It is a plea for a more benevolent and cooperative attitude toward people of all denominations who are a part of the family of God. And, if not more benevolence and cooperation, at least more tolerance.

On February 3, 1943, the transport *Dorchester* was torpedoed off the coast of Greenland. As the ship went down, four chaplains, all of different denominations, were on deck passing out life preservers. When there were no life preservers left, they gave their own away. The chaplains were last seen standing arm in arm praying.

They went to their deaths, united in the service of a common Lord. Our world waits today for Christians of all denominations to lock their arms together in peace and love and be willing to die serving and reaching others.